LINGUISTIC SURVEYS OF AFRICA

Volume 11

THE CLASSIFICATION OF THE
BANTU LANGUAGES
bound with
BANTU WORD DIVISION

THE CLASSIFICATION OF THE BANTU LANGUAGES

MALCOLM GUTHRIE

LONDON AND NEW YORK

First published in 1948 by Oxford University Press

This edition first published in 2018
by Routledge
2 Park Square, Milton Park, Abingdon, Oxon OX14 4RN

and by Routledge
711 Third Avenue, New York, NY 10017

Routledge is an imprint of the Taylor & Francis Group, an informa business

© 1948 International African Institute 1948

All rights reserved. No part of this book may be reprinted or reproduced or utilised in any form or by any electronic, mechanical, or other means, now known or hereafter invented, including photocopying and recording, or in any information storage or retrieval system, without permission in writing from the publishers.

Trademark notice: Product or corporate names may be trademarks or registered trademarks, and are used only for identification and explanation without intent to infringe.

British Library Cataloguing-in-Publication Data
A catalogue record for this book is available from the British Library

ISBN: 978-1-138-08975-4 (Set)
ISBN: 978-1-315-10381-5 (Set) (ebk)
ISBN: 978-1-138-09582-3 (Volume 11) (hbk)
ISBN: 978-1-138-09585-4 (Volume 11) (pbk)
ISBN: 978-1-315-10553-6 (Volume 11) (ebk)

Publisher's Note
The publisher has gone to great lengths to ensure the quality of this reprint but points out that some imperfections in the original copies may be apparent.

Disclaimer
The publisher has made every effort to trace copyright holders and would welcome correspondence from those they have been unable to trace.

Due to modern production methods, it has not been possible to reproduce the fold-out maps within the book. Please visit www.routledge.com to view them.

THE CLASSIFICATION
OF THE
BANTU LANGUAGES

BY

MALCOLM GUTHRIE

Published for the
INTERNATIONAL AFRICAN INSTITUTE
by the
OXFORD UNIVERSITY PRESS
LONDON NEW YORK TORONTO
1948

Oxford University Press, Amen House, London E.C. 4
GLASGOW NEW YORK TORONTO MELBOURNE WELLINGTON
BOMBAY CALCUTTA MADRAS CAPE TOWN
Geoffrey Cumberlege, Publisher to the University

This study is one of a series of publications issued in connexion with the Handbook of African Languages which the International African Institute is preparing with the aid of a grant made by the Secretary of State under the Colonial Development and Welfare Acts, on the recommendation of the Colonial Social Science Research Council.

PRINTED IN GREAT BRITAIN

CHAPTER I
INTRODUCTION

THE latter half of the nineteenth century saw the end of most of the great exploratory journeys into that part of Africa which lies to the south of the Equator. The expansion of missionary work which followed on the opening up of the previously unknown areas during this period gave rise to intense interest in the languages of the newly discovered peoples. This resulted in the production of a surprising number of dictionaries and grammars describing the various languages which were found.

As early as 1862 Bleek drew the attention of scholars to the fact that there was a startling family resemblance between widely separated languages in this area. When more grammars became available it became evident that the Bantu family was indeed a very large one. Moreover, its peculiar characteristics have been of considerable interest to linguistic students in other fields. Up to this time not a few of the languages have been fairly completely documented, while one or two have received special attention. This is particularly so in the case of the work of Doke on Zulu, and of Laman on Kongo, to mention only two cases in which such studies have reached a high level.

Nevertheless, there are still two things to be done in this field. No satisfactory method of classification has yet been developed for this great number of clearly related languages. In addition there is still no work of reference from which research workers may know where are the principal gaps in our knowledge. The recently published bibliography of Bantu by Doke has given us a very useful book, in which is set out in considerable detail an account of the works so far published on the various members of the Bantu family of languages. As part of the framework of his monograph Doke used a broad classification based on certain features chosen for the purpose. What he did not do, because it would have been outside the scope of the work, was to give us any complete picture of what is known about the whole family, or to make any reference to the many languages which have no documentation. To achieve this it is necessary to survey the whole field in a different way, and that is what this present work sets out to do.

The aim of this monograph then is twofold. It is intended first of all to establish some framework which may serve for future reference in identifying and classifying Bantu languages. Then in the second place, as an important by-product, it will throw into prominence the places where our knowledge is fragmentary or even non-existent.

The important thing to bear in mind when consulting this work is that the classification is essentially tentative. In a few areas, where our data are reasonably adequate, the grouping may lay claim to a certain amount of finality. In many cases, however, where whole sets of languages are known chiefly as names only, the classification is necessarily experimental, and must not be taken as authoritative in any way.

In some cases the conclusion reached from fragmentary data will probably be found to be only partially correct. It is hoped, however, that the publication of this tentative work will stimulate any who are in a position to do so to contribute more complete information on the subject. In other cases little-known languages have been grouped together because a supposed relationship has been asserted by some earlier writer.

It may well be that those who have direct contact with these languages possess data which show that such grouping is unjustified. Here, too, the co-operation of such workers will be appreciated, since it is desirable that in any subsequent edition the needful revisions should be made. In this way the setting out of all that can be known from the available data, however inconclusive, will have served its purpose.

The Plan of the Work

There are four principal parts to this study. In the first we shall investigate the questions arising out of the use of the term Bantu. Among other things this involves establishing and illustrating the criteria to be used in identifying languages as members of the Bantu family. The following chapter is then devoted to a discussion of the various aspects of the problems of classification. Chief among these is the method to be adopted in attempting to classify the Bantu languages. Then in Chapter IV the technique which has been described is applied, and its results shown in the form of a series of descriptive classifications of each of the principal areas in turn. Finally there is a map, together with a key in the form of a complete list of the languages classified in their groups.

One difficulty that had to be faced arose from the fact that some languages have been called by more than one name. This has been dealt with in two ways. In general the name accepted as correct is that used by the speakers of a language to refer to it. Where the name has a class prefix, the usual practice is followed of omitting this prefix, and where, as in the case of MWADGA (known as **iciinamwaŋga**), the name is preceded by the word **iciina** 'the language of the people of', this is naturally not used. The element **-nya-** which occurs in some names, e.g. NYADKOLE (called **olunyaŋkole**), is retained, since its meaning is obscure, and sometimes it has become universally recognized as part of the word, e.g. it would be of small value to call NYAMWESI by the shortened form MWESI. In the full list of languages accompanying the map, the other names which have been used for a given language are placed in parentheses, and then at the end of the work there is an alphabetical index to all the names. It would clearly have been neither practicable nor useful to give all the spelling variants of certain names, so a peculiar spelling is only noted if it alters the position of the word in the index.

In the fourth chapter a system of numeration is developed by means of which any language may be referred to by a letter and two figures. Since this also enables any language to be found on the map, the numbering is given in parentheses after the name, each time a language is mentioned, even before the significance of the numeration has been explained.

Orthography

In any study of the Bantu languages in general the problem of orthography becomes very difficult. It is clear that the considerations governing the designing of a practical orthography do not necessarily operate in this case. On the other hand, to use any system of spelling that did not conform in most respects to the orthography based on the 'Africa' alphabet would be unsatisfactory, while to depart too much from the conventional spelling of important languages would in itself reduce the usefulness of the work.

One of the biggest difficulties in a general study of the Bantu languages arises from the existence of five-vowel languages side by side with the seven-vowel languages. On the one hand it would be misleading to represent identical pronunciation differently in different languages, but on the other the spelling of one language can hardly be determined by the characteristics of its neighbours. Fortunately the most serious aspect of this problem has been overcome by the recent development of the 'Africa' alphabet to include a system of nine vowel characters. This has meant that the two new characters i̧ and u̧ could be used for the extra close vowels of the seven-vowel languages. As a result of this, those who only know the traditional five-vowel symbol system in the seven-vowel languages of East Africa will easily recognize the spelling, as will those who have no acquaintance with other than five-vowel languages. For the seven-vowel languages of the north and north-west, however, the spelling of the words has had to be adapted. There can be little doubt that the seven vowel characters of the original 'Africa' alphabet are the most suitable for any practical orthography of these languages, but clearly in a work which covers the whole of the Bantu field consistency must mean slight inconvenience in certain cases. Anyone using this work who has been accustomed to the open vowel characters will therefore have to interpret the spelling in this way: i̧ = i, i = e, e = ɛ, u̧ = u, u = o, o = ɔ. It must be emphasized, however, that the use of the new letters implies no suggestion that they would be suitable for general use in these particular languages. As already stated, it seems reasonably certain that the use of the two open vowel characters is the most satisfactory thing for them.

Another problem in a work of this kind is how to write fricative consonants. It would not be practicable to use the special symbol in every case, especially as it frequently happens that the exact nature of the articulation is unimportant. For example, in BEMBA (M.42a) there is only one voiced bilabial consonant, and the fact that it is fricative in a word like **abantu** 'people' would in no sense justify the use of a special character. When we come to other languages, however, such as MBUNDU (R.11), there is the difficulty that an identical sound, which has an almost identical value in the language, is written 'v', e.g. **ovandu** 'people'. Such a spelling could not be used in this work, but in view of its existence there does arise the necessity for indicating that the sound in such words is a simple fricative bilabial. Purely as an expedient for our present purpose, therefore, and in no way supporting the undesirable practice of using such diacritics in current orthographies, any sound which is known to be fricative will be represented by the character for the plosive underlined, e.g. ḇ = β (v in the 'Africa' alphabet), p̱ = ɸ (f in the 'Africa' alphabet), ḵ = x, g̱ = ɣ.

The symbols **c** and **j** have been used consistently throughout to represent either palatal plosives or simple affricates of the type tʃ, dʒ. Although this involves the use of the same character for quite different sounds, the fact is that in many cases we do not really know which of the two sounds occurs, and so it is convenient not to have to distinguish them in the spelling.

In the case of ʃ and ʒ the problem is somewhat similar, except that here we do not know whether these sounds are essentially distinct from **s** and **z** respectively. To use the phonetic symbols for them would frequently mean introducing an extra character unnecessarily, and would also obscure the relationship between words in different languages. For this reason the symbols ʂ and ʐ have been adopted, since they will also cover the possibility of other palatalized fricatives such as ç and ʑ.

The usual method of representing dental sounds presents several problems, and on the whole seems unsatisfactory for our present purpose. As a tentative measure, then, the fact that a sound has a dental pronunciation will be shown by the placing of a cedilla beneath it. This means that θ can be written ş, and in some cases this is most useful, especially where words with θ in some languages appear with s in others. Where θ is not related to an s in other languages, as in KELE (A.73) the phonetic symbol is retained for the dental fricative, but only in these cases.

The character ŋ for the velar nasal is required in the case of a number of languages, such as FAD (A.66), where it represents a sound that has to be distinguished from ŋg. For this reason it has been used throughout as the nasal in compounds with velar consonants, even in those languages where to do so in a practical orthography would be an unnecessary complication. This is simply because it is desirable that similar words should be spelt identically in different languages in a study of this kind.

The question of word-division hardly enters into the scope of this present work. It must be pointed out, however, that the grammatical system which is presupposed throughout the work demands what would be called a 'conjunctive' system of writing. Consequently in none of the examples cited is any regard paid to the current practice of word-division in force in the language in question. This is not to be interpreted as any premature pronouncement on the matter, where a language happens to be written more or less disjunctively, but merely as an attempt to achieve grammatical consistency.

DATA

Much of the information needed for this study has had to be derived from observations made by other people. Inevitably this means that the reliability of the data collected in such a way is extremely variable. In some cases, too, further research may show that certain conclusions are invalid through their having been based on statements that were misleading rather than incorrect. Such, however, are the limitations due to the inadequacy of our present knowledge of the Bantu field.

In some respects, however, the present work may claim to have a certain distinctiveness, since I have been fortunate enough to be able to gather a very large proportion of the data at first hand. It so happens that the only area where I have had no personal contact with any of the languages is the one I call Zone A. Everything said about the languages of this region therefore has had to be taken from the work of others and is of indeterminate reliability. In much of Zone T also are languages concerning which I have had to rely on what others have told me or have stated in their published works. The net result of this is that of the languages illustrated in the chapter dealing with criteria the only ones I have not personally studied on the field are FAD (A.66) and RODGA (T.24), while in the chapter on differentia every example given has either been obtained from or verified by native speakers of the language in question.

The map at the end suffers from the same disabilities as the rest of the work. Every effort has been made to check all the available data in order to fix the geographical limits of each language, but our knowledge is extremely patchy. Some areas, such as Southern Rhodesia, which has been accurately surveyed by Doke, are well known, but others such as the Portuguese colonies still need much research before we can be sure that our linguistic maps are reliable. Taking it over all the map is probably about 50 per cent. accurate, a figure which is almost certainly higher than that for any existing map.

CHAPTER II

IDENTIFYING THE BANTU LANGUAGES

BEFORE the problem of classification can be discussed, it is clearly necessary to determine what is meant by the term Bantu. Fortunately from the time this name was first introduced it has chiefly been applied to linguistic rather than to ethnological facts. This makes it quite suitable for our present purpose, and justifies our attempting to define it linguistically.

It is to Bleek that we owe the term, which he spelt Bâ-ntu in the first part of his *Comparative Grammar*. When he produced the second part of this work seven years later in 1869, he dropped the hyphen, but still retained the accent, apparently because he considered that this was necessary for the correct orthography of Xhosa, from which language he adopted the term. From that time this name has become accepted for this remarkable family of languages spoken over much of central and southern Africa.

It is interesting to reflect that Bleek did not attempt any close definition of the term Bantu, contenting himself with what he termed the 'main distinctive features' of the languages. All he did in fact was to point out that the specific languages he was examining had certain features in common, which were, to quote his words (the italics being his), 'a concord of the *pronouns* and of every part of speech, in the formation of which pronouns are employed (e.g. adjectives and verbs) *with the nouns* to which they respectively refer, and the hereby caused *distribution of the nouns into classes or genders*'. Had he continued to study this family he would no doubt have given us some criteria by means of which the languages belonging to it might be distinguished from others which do not. In his day, however, there was not enough known about the languages of central Africa to make this a pressing problem.

Subsequent writers have been principally concerned with typical features rather than with true criteria. The consequence of this is that few if any of them have defined what they mean when they say that a given language is Bantu. It would be of small value to cite in full the lists of the features as given by different people. Instead the principal references will be given first and then afterwards some comments.

After Bleek the next outstanding writer to interest himself in the Bantu family was Lepsius, in the introduction to his *Nubische Grammatik*, 1880. He set out twelve propositions which were intended to show the peculiar characteristics of the Bantu family. These were subsequently quoted in a somewhat condensed form by Cust in his *Sketch of the Modern Languages of Africa*, 1883. Long after this the propositions of Lepsius were considered to be an authoritative outline of Bantu criteria, being used by Werner in *The Bantu Languages* as late as 1919. The last and most important citation of them is a critical one in Johnstone's great work, *A Comparative Study of the Bantu and Semi-Bantu Languages*, 1919, to which those interested should refer

In 1891 Torrend published his *Comparative Grammar of the South-African Bantu Languages*, in which he treats at length of what he calls the 'characteristic features' of the family. Of his four principles, however, only the first has much value, and this is simply a restatement of the system of prefix concord. He gives nothing at all which might help towards a delimitation of Bantu.

Five years later there appeared *Études sur les langues du Haut-Zambézie* by Jacottet, a work which contains a considerable introduction dealing with general questions arising in the field of Bantu language study. Curiously enough, however, he makes no attempt whatever to define what he means by Bantu, apparently assuming that his readers already know.

Another interesting thing is that Meinhof, to whom the subject of Bantu philology owes so much, does not seem to have attempted any definition of the term Bantu. Presumably he was content to take its meaning as being sufficiently clear.

Johnstone, in the work already referred to, sets out twelve propositions of his own 'to define the special or peculiar features of the Bantu languages', at the same time as showing why he does not accept the propositions of Lepsius. Although some of his features are of wider application than those of any previous list, yet they have a real weakness which arises from the inadequate grammatical and phonetic technique at the disposal of the writer.

Other writers have also dealt with this question, without making any important contribution to the subject, since they mostly reiterate what has been said previously. In 1935, however, Doke published his well-known *Bantu Linguistic Terminology*, in which he sets out eleven main characteristics of Bantu languages. This is a much clearer statement than any that had previously been made, but here again the features are not given as criteria, and so do not meet our demand for some means of deciding whether or not a given language is to be taken as Bantu.

Finally Tucker in his *Eastern Sudanic Languages*, 1940, gives a well-set-out statement of what he calls 'criteria ... for comparison with Sudanic and Hamitic languages'. In point of fact the seventeen characteristics listed have been chosen principally to fit in with the lists the author had already established for Semitic and Hamitic languages, and as he notes 'there are other Bantu criteria which fall outside these seventeen points and which would accordingly need a separate treatment in a Bantu exposition'.

One thing which becomes evident from a study of all these lists is that nobody has so far established any real criteria which can be applied to a language to discover whether it would fall within the Bantu family or not. The most that has been achieved is a more or less complete statement of the characteristic features of Bantu languages, scarcely any one of which is found to apply to all the languages which everyone has accepted as Bantu. Thus, for example, most writers emphasize certain phonetic characteristics such as open syllables, but in Luwunda (L.52) there are such forms as **diyal** 'stone', and **cikas** 'hand', while many languages in Zones A and B have such forms as **osal** 'to work' and **osip** 'to strike'. It is no answer to this problem to suggest that the final vowel has been lost through the influence of non-Bantu languages, since languages with words like these are either to be included in or excluded from the Bantu family. If they are to be included, then the open syllable cannot be a criterion.

Johnstone also says that 'No two consonants can come together without an intervening vowel, except one of them to be an aspirate or a nasal, and no consonant is doubled in pronunciation'. That this is of little value is shown by the fact that he himself gives words which break these rules, as **bgato** 'canoe' and **sxwa** 'termite' in Karanga (his No. 64), and **murro** 'fire' in Copi (his No. 2b) and **edziǵǵa** (this incorrectly for ezziǵa) 'tear' in Ganda (his No. 4). Other phonetic features such as stress and tone are often mentioned, but it can be shown that in LUBA-LULUA (L.31) and BEMBA

(M.42a) there is no stress of any kind, and that in NYIKYŲSA (M.31) and MAKUA (P.31) there are no tones.

Various grammatical features are also cited, such as the existence of 'object infixes' or 'verb species', but in Zones A and B there are languages which have all the other recognized Bantu characteristics, but neither of these.

The problem confronting us then is the establishing of clear criteria by which the use of the term Bantu can be defined. One of the prerequisites for these is a grammatical system within which the criteria may operate. There is no space in this present work for me to develop such a system, but the following suggestions for criteria must be taken to be an integral part of the system. Any slight obscurity that may appear to inhere in the definitions will be due to this fact, though it is probable that this may be dispelled when the reader has studied the next chapter.

The Criteria

It is necessary to divide into two groups the criteria to be used for identifying languages as Bantu. This is because there are some languages in which contraction and attrition have to be postulated to such an extent that it becomes extremely difficult to apply some of the criteria. These are therefore placed in the second group and labelled 'subsidiary'. The use of this term is not, however, to be taken to mean that the criteria in this group are less important, simply that they are less easy to apply.

Here then is a bare list of the criteria. This is followed by examples chosen to illustrate each of them in turn.

A. *Principal Criteria*

1. A system of grammatical genders, usually at least five, with these features:

   (*a*) The sign of gender is a prefix, by means of which words may be assorted into a number of classes varying roughly from ten to twenty.

   (*b*) There is a regular association of pairs of classes to indicate the singular and plural of the genders. In addition to these two-class genders, there are also one-class genders where the prefix is sometimes similar to one of the singular prefixes occurring in a two-class gender, and sometimes similar to one of the plural prefixes.

   (*c*) When a word has an independent prefix as the sign of its class, any other word which is subordinate to it has to agree with it as to class by means of a dependent prefix.

   (*d*) There is no correlation of the genders with sex reference or with any other clearly defined idea.

2. A vocabulary, part of which can be related by fixed rules to a set of hypothetical common roots.

B. *Subsidiary Criteria*

3. A set of invariable cores, or radicals, from which almost all words are formed by an agglutinative process, these radicals having the following features:

   (*a*) They are composed of Consonant-Vowel-Consonant.

   (*b*) When a grammatical suffix is attached to the radical there is formed a 'base' on which words identifiable as 'verbals' are built.

(c) When a non-grammatical, or lexical, suffix is attached to the radical there is formed a 'stem' on which words identifiable as nominals are built. When a nominal belongs to a two-class gender the sounds and tones of the stem are the same in both classes.

(d) A radical may be extended by an element found between it and the suffix. Such elements, termed 'extensions', are composed either of Vowel-Consonant or of a single vowel.

(e) The only case of a radical occurring without a prefix of any kind occurs in verbals used as interjections.

4. A balanced vowel system in the radicals, consisting of one open vowel 'a' with an equal number of back and front vowels.

Examples of the Criteria

1. *The Grammatical Genders*

(a) *The Classes*. It might seem rather superfluous to illustrate a feature so well known as this, but even if only for the sake of completeness some examples must be given. Here then are lists of type words with independent prefix, taken from seven widely separated languages. For clearness the prefixes are shown separated by hyphens.

A. FAŊ (A.66). 1. **mu-r** 'person'. 2. **bu-neɡa** 'women'. 3. **m-bį** 'door'. 4. **mį-nlu** 'heads'. 5. **a-kok̲** 'stone'. 6. **me-lų** 'days'. 7. **i-ku** 'skin'. 8. **bį-vį** 'bones'. 9. **n-dam** 'width'. 10. **u-nyų** 'finger'.

B. BUBAŊGĮ (C.21b). 1. **mu-yįbį** 'thief'. 2. **ba-kunzį** 'chiefs'. 3. **mu-kolo** 'night'. 4. **mį-luku** 'hearts'. 5. **lį-kabu** 'gift'. 6. **ma-boko** 'arms'. 7. **i-lamba** 'cloth'. 8. **bį-saŋga** 'islands'. 9. **n-tįna** 'root'. 10. **n-cete** 'nails'. 11. **lu-kulu** 'leg'. 12. **bu-lįtu** 'weight'.

C. ĮLAMBA (F.31). 1. **umu-nuna** 'brother'. 2. **ia-suŋgu** 'wives'. 3. **umu-ɡunda** 'garden'. 4. **imi-kono** 'arms'. 5. **į-kota** 'tree'. 6. **ima-lolo** 'mud'. 7. **iki-muli** 'torch'. 8. **įį-ndolo** 'potatoes'. 9. **in-zila** 'path'. 10. **įn-sįmba** 'lions'. 11. **ulu-limį** 'tongue'. 12. **ika-ɡii** 'small egg'. 13. **įpį-tįįla** 'small cloths'. 14. **uu-ta** 'bow'. 15. **kuį-ɡenda** 'going'.

D. RUGURU (G.35). 1. **imu-ana** 'child'. 2. **iwa-lume** 'men'. 3. **ɡum-biki** 'tree'. 4. **imi-ɡunda** 'gardens'. 5. **-baɡo** 'grass'. 6. **ɡama-bue** 'stones'. 7. **iki-sima** 'well'. 8. **ipfi-moka** 'potatoes'. 9. **im-buli** 'debt'. 10. **tsin-sabi** 'ropes'. 11. **ulu-kuli** 'body'. 12. **u-beho** 'wind'. 13. **ila-tsoka** 'small snake'. 14. **uku-sona** 'sewing'.

E. B̲EMBA (M.42a). 1. **umu-kasi** 'wife'. 2. **aba-londo** 'fishermen'. 3. **umu-peni** 'knife'. 4. **imi-fuko** 'sacks'. 5. **i-b̲ala** 'garden'. 6. **ama-tipa** 'mud'. 7. **ici-puna** 'stool'. 8. **ifi-lamba** 'tears'. 9. **in-supa** 'calabash'. 10. **in-seko** 'laughter'. 11. **ulu-limi** 'tongue'. 12. **aka-sub̲a** 'sun'. 13. **utu-mini** 'centipedes'. 14. **ub̲u-lalo** 'bridge'. 15. **uku-tui** 'ear'. 16. **apa-ntu** 'precise place'. 17. **umu-ntu** 'enclosed place'.

F. MBUNDU (R.11). 1. **u-lume** 'man'. 2. **ob̲a-pika** 'slaves'. 3. **u-tale** 'iron'. 4. **ob̲i-tima** 'hearts'. 5. **e-limi** 'tongue'. 6. **a-b̲ele** 'breasts'. 7. **oci-nɡumba** 'thief'. 8. **om-bisi** 'fish'. 9. **olon-jila** 'paths'. 10. **olu-nye** 'fly'. 11. **oka-luŋga** 'sea'. 12. **otu-b̲alu** 'horses'. 13. **o-wuya** 'heat'. 14. **oku-ulu** 'leg'.

G. ROŊGA (T.24).   1. amu-tiri 'worker'.   2. aba-fambi 'travellers'.   3. an-tiro 'work'.   4. ami-lambu 'rivers'.   5. a-lapi 'rag'.   6. ama-siku 'days'.   7. aʃi-kosi 'neck'.   8. apsi-komu 'axes'.   9. am-bilu 'heart'.   10. atin-siba 'feathers'.   11. ali-bambu 'rib'.   12. abu-kulu 'greatness'.   13. aku-famba 'going'.

Since this is not a work on Comparative Bantu, no attempt has been made to correlate the numbering of the classes in the different languages. Moreover, where there are other forms of the one prefix, as, for example, with a monosyllabic stem, these are not shown. Similarly, since we are considering grammatical form and not etymology, it is of no importance that the word **otubalu** (Mbundu Class 12) is apparently the plural of a loan-word **okabalu** 'horse' (cf. Portuguese *cavallo*).

(*b*) *2-Class and 1-Class Genders*. This feature has not received the clarity of treatment in the past that it should have done. For this reason it must be adequately illustrated. The following lists of the two types of genders are from the same seven languages, but it must not be assumed that they are exhaustive, since other genders may well exist in some of these.

A. FAŊ (A.66)

1/2	mu-nega/ba-nega 'woman, women'	3.	m-bon 'oil'
3/4	n-lem/mį-nlem 'heart(s)'	4.	mį-ya 'entrails'
5/6	a-lo/me-lo 'ear(s)'	5.	a-kųma 'honour'
7/8	i-to/bį-to 'cloth(s)'	6.	me-kįį 'blood'
9/6	n-da/me-nda 'house(s)'	7.	i-kįį 'strength'
10/5	u-non/a-non 'bird(s)'	8.	bį-su 'dispute'
		9.	m-bįla 'speed'
		10.	u-son 'shame'

B. BUBAŊGĮ (C.21b)

1/2	mu-nįŋga/ba-nįŋga 'friend(s)'	2.	ba-tųbį 'excreta'
3/4	mu-sulu/mį-sulu 'stream(s)'	3.	mu-lįka 'mercy'
5/6	lį-bele/ma-bele 'breast(s)'	4.	mį-tukį 'sweat'
5/2	lį-kutu/ba-kutu 'smallpox pustule(s)'	5.	lį-kįndį 'aroma'
5/4	lį-ulu (pr. zulu)/mį-ulu 'nose(s)'	6.	ma-lolų 'jelly'
7/8	i-loko/bį-loko 'thing(s)'	7.	i-lunga 'innocence'
7/2	i-yele/ba-yele 'bullet(s)'	8.	bį-lukįsa 'rust'
9/10	n-kįŋgu/n-kįŋgu 'neck(s)'	9.	m-pįo 'cold'
9/6	n-kumbu/ma-nkumbu 'nickname(s)'	10.	n-golį 'sleep'
		11.	lu-bįku 'permanence'
11/6	lu-boko/ma-boko 'arm(s)'	12.	bu-lulu 'bitterness'
11/10	lu-pusu/m-pusu 'skin(s)'		
12/6	bu-tali/ma-tali 'knife(s)'		

C. ĮLAMBA (F.31)

1/2	umu-tepį/ia-tepį 'thief(s)'	3.	umu-lamu 'quietness'
3/4	umu-gulu/imi-gulu 'leg(s)'	4.	imi-garį 'blood'
5/6	į-kųpa/ima-kųpa 'bone(s)'	5.	į-gulo 'sky'
7/8	iki-latu/įį-latu 'shoe(s)'	6.	ima-kųta 'oil'

THE CLASSIFICATION OF

C. ỊLAMBA (F.31) (contd.)

7/6 iki-kololo/ima-kololo 'cough(s)'
9/10 in-sịme/ịn-sịme 'knife(s)'
11/10 ulu-tondo/in-tondo 'day(s)'
11/6 ulu-tụmbi/ima-tụmbi 'hair(s)'
12/13 ika-nanso/ịpị-nanso 'little girl(s)'

7. iki-kima 'female habits'
8. ịị-gao 'bread'
9. in-zala 'hunger'
10. ịn-guru 'power'
11. ulu-nkundi 'dust'
12. ika-uloa 'feeble love'
13. ịpị-sala 'insufficient wisdom'
14. uu-kata 'laziness'
15. kuị-genda 'going'

D. RUGURU (G.35)

1/2 im-zungu/iwa-zungu 'European(s)'
3/4 gum-gulu/imi-gulu 'leg(s)'
5/6 -fiŋga/gama-fiŋga 'egg(s)'
5a/4 di-guku/imi-guku 'big fowl(s)'
7/8 iki-goda/ipfi-goda 'stool(s)'
9/10 iŋ-guku/tsiŋ-guku 'fowl(s)'
11/10 ulu-limi/tsin-dimi 'tongue(s)'
11/4 ulu-goŋgo/imi-goŋgo 'hill(s)'
12/6 u-lili/gama-lili 'bed(s)'
13/8 ila-mage/ipfi-mage 'small knife(s)'

3. gum-lopa 'blood'
4. imi-saŋga 'sand'
5. -woga 'fear'
6. gama-kala 'charcoal'
8. ipfi-pfuta 'little oil'
10. im-beho 'cold'
11. u-tulo 'sleep'
13. uku-zeŋga 'building'

E. ḄEMBA (M.42a)

1/2 umu-lume/aḅa-lume 'husband(s)'
3/4 umu-ḅili/imi-ḅili 'body(s)'
5/6 i-sembe/ama-sembe 'axe(s)'
7/8 ici-londa/ifi-londa 'wound(s)'
9/10 in-soka/in-soka 'snake'
9/6 in-noŋgo/ama-loŋgo 'pot(s)'
11/10 ulu-sato/in-sato 'python(s)'
11/6 ulu-kasa/ama-kasa 'sole(s)'
12/13 aka-tende/utu-tende 'heel(s)'
14/6 uḅu-tanda/ama-tanda 'mat(s)'
15/6 uku-ḅoko/ama-ḅoko 'arm(s)'

1a. makanta 'locust(s)'
3. umu-lopa 'blood'
4. imi-pembu 'refreshment'
5. i-loḅa 'earth'
6. ama-saka 'kaffir-corn'
7. ici-ani 'grass'
8. ifi-basi 'leprosy'
9. in-sala 'hunger'
10. in-soni 'shame'
11. ulu-ḅilo 'speed'
12. aka-pumpu 'insolence'
13. utu-lo 'sleep'
14. uḅu-luŋgu 'bead(s)'
15. uku-pita 'passing'
16. apa-ntu 'precise place'
17. umu-ntu 'enclosed place'

F. MBUNDU (R.11)

1/2 u-feko/oḅa-feko 'girl(s)'
3/4 u-kolo/oḅi-kolo 'rope(s)'
5/6 e-sala/a-sala 'egg(s)'
7/4 oci-lapo/oḅi-lapo 'paddle(s)'
8/9 oŋ-golo/oloŋ-golo 'knee(s)'

3. u-sumba 'fear'
4. oḅi-nene 'rubbish'
5. e-seke 'sand'
6. a-loḅa 'mud'
7. oci-sola 'love'

F. MBUNDU (R.11) (contd.)

   10/9 olu-sapo/olo-sapo 'fable(s)'
   11/12 oka-pote/otu-pote 'coat(s)'
   13/6 o-wato/a-wato 'canoe(s)'
   14/6 oku-oko/oba-oko 'arm(s)'

   8. on-dulu 'gall'
   9. olon-jele 'beard'
   10. olu-me 'dew'
   11. oka-soŋgu 'bead(s)'
   12. otu-ma 'clay'
   13. o-wisi 'smoke'

G. RODGA (T.24)

   1/2 amu-yibi/aba-yibi 'thief(s)'
   3/4 am-pimu/ami-pimu 'measure(s)'
   5/6 a-boko/ama-boko 'arm(s)'
   7/8 aʃi-lembe/apsi-lembe 'hat(s)'
   9/10 am-buti/atim-buti 'goat(s)'
   11/10 ali-bala/atim-bala 'plain(s)'
   12/6 abu-gamu/ama-gamu 'end(s)'

   3. an-talo 'abundance'
   4. ami-saba 'earth'
   6. ama-golo 'greediness'
   7. aʃi-rami 'cold'
   9. am-bere 'dew'
   10. atin-tʃalu 'kindness'
   11. ali-sima 'price'
   12. abu-lolo 'laziness'

It will be noted that the one class genders cannot be equated with any notional category like 'abstract' or 'substance', but that countable words like 'bead(s)' and 'locust(s)' may be found in them.

From the examples given it is clear that no attempt can be made to associate one set of prefixes with the idea of 'singular' and another with 'plural'. This is not only because of the one-class genders but also because of the fact that one class may be plural in one gender and singular in another, as in FAD 5/6 and 10/5.

(c) *Agreement by Dependent Prefixes*. To illustrate this criterion two sentences are given from each of the seven type languages. The English equivalent is the same in each case, and one of the sentences is the plural corresponding to the other. The meaning is 'his other knife is lost' and 'his other knives are lost'. In this case also the prefixes are separated by hyphens simply to throw them into relief, though they are naturally an integral part of the word.

FAD (A.66)	u-keŋ by-a m-box u-ŋgazįme
	a-keŋ dy-a a-vox e-ŋgazįme
BUBADGĮ (C.21b)	bu-tali bu-yiyi bu-sįsu bu-ulįmbana
	ma-tali ma-yiyi ma-sįsu ma-ulįmbana
ĮLAMBA (F.31)	in-sįme y-akwe y-iŋgi i-lįmilįle
	įn-sįme z-akwe z-iŋgi zį-lįlimįle
RUGURU (G.35)	gum-mage gw-ake m-yage gw-agire
	imi-mage y-ake mi-yage y-agire
BEMBA (M.42a)	umu-peni u-akue u-mbi naa-u-luba
	imi-peni i-akue i-mbi naa-i-luba
MBUNDU (R.11)	om-moko y-ahe yi-kwabo y-anyelela
	olom-moko by-ahe bi-kwabo by-anyelela
RODGA (T.24)	amu-kwa w-akwe wu-ŋwana wu-lalekile
	ami-kwa y-akwe yi-ŋwana mi-lalekile

The most important feature of this prefix agreement is simply that there is a dependent prefix corresponding to each independent prefix. The term 'alliterative concord' has frequently been used, but from these few examples it will be seen that this is hardly an adequate description of the facts. It is therefore preferable not to use it, but simply to speak of agreement by prefixes.

(*d*) *Absence of Correlation of Genders and Ideas.* Since this is a negative criterion it is difficult to illustrate. Here, however, are some examples from BEMBA which will demonstrate that there is not necessarily a correlation even between gender and the idea of person.

Here are a few typical examples chosen from the large number that might be given.

tumba umutali 'a long skin bag'
baatumba abatali 'long skin bags'

This shows that the prefixes **umu-/aba-** are not confined to personal reference.

isilu ilitali 'a tall madman'
amasilu ayatali 'tall madmen'
icibambe icitali 'a tall hunter'
ifibambe ifitali 'tall hunters'

These show that other genders may also refer to persons, and so cannot be said to be confined to things and non-personal living creatures.

2. *The Related Vocabulary*

To illustrate this criterion adequately would require a treatise on Comparative Bantu, but its importance and application may be seen in the following examples from MFINU (B.41). This language is remarkable in having upwards of twelve simple vowels, including three **u**-sounds and three **o**-sounds. Here are examples of words containing these sounds, together with the starred forms of common Bantu to which they can be related.

With very close **u**	**ndu** 'pepper'	*-LUNGU (cf. BUBAŊGĮ: nduŋgu)
	bbu 'beach'	*-BUNGU (cf. BUBAŊGĮ: ḷḁbuŋgu)
With open **u**	**mpu** 'rat'	*-PUKU (cf. KOŊGO: mpuku)
	ndu 'brother'	*-LUGU (cf. KOŊGO: nduku)
With very open **u**	**ntu** 'chest'	*-TULU (cf. BUBAŊGĮ: ntulu)
	ndu 'bile'	*-LULU (cf. BUBAŊGĮ: ndulu)
With close **o**	**oko** 'to pull'	*-KOK- (cf. KOŊGO: koka)
	olo 'to bewitch'	*-LOG- (cf. BUBAŊGĮ: loko)
With open **o**	**obo** 'to rot'	*-BOL- (cf. BUBAŊGĮ: bolo)
	tto 'sleep'	*-TOLO (cf. KOŊGO: tolo)
With very open **o**	**ndo** 'affair'	*-LAGA (cf. BUBAŊGĮ: ilaka)
	obo 'to get'	*-BAK- (cf. KOŊGO: baka)

From these few but typical examples it may be seen that a certain quality of vowel in monosyllabic stems in MFINU is correlated to a given type of second consonant in the starred form. In this way a definite, even if unusual, relationship of vocabulary is established for this language.

3. Word-Building from Radicals

The first and last words of the singular sentences given above may be taken in order to illustrate the first of the subsidiary criteria. To throw the radicals into relief they are put in the upper case, while the grammatical suffixes are separated by a hyphen. The extensions are in the lower case but may be known in the verbals in that they are not separated from the radical.

```
FAŊ (A.66)        uKEŊ uŋgaZĮMe (i.e. Ext. -e)
BUBAŊGĮ (C.21b)   buTALi buuLĮMBan-a (i.e. Ext. -an-)
ĮLAMBA (F.31)     inSIMe iLĮMil-įle (i.e. Ext. -il-)
RUGURU (G.35)     ġumMAGe ġwAG-ire
BEMBA (M.42a)     umuPENi naauLUB-a
MBUNDU (R.11)     omMOKo yaNYELel-a (i.e. Ext. -el-)
ROŊGA (T.24)      amuKUa wuLALek-ile (i.e. Ext. -ek-)
```

The example from FAŊ shows the difficulty of applying subsidiary criteria, since neither of the words in this language has a suffix. In spite of this, however, the radical has a structure similar to those of the other languages.

To illustrate still further the way in which the radical occurs in words of both kinds, here are some groups of words from five of the languages.

FAŊ: -LŲK 'marry' (with grammatical suffix, -LŲG-a)
         -LŲGe 'arrange marriage of'   aLŲK/meLŲK 'marriage(s)'

BUBAŊGĮ: -BAL- 'marry'   -BALįs- 'give in marriage'
         -BALil- 'assist at marriage of'
         lįBALa/maBALa 'marriage(s)'
         muBALilį/baBALilį 'assistant(s) at marriage'

ĮLAMBA: -TOOL- 'marry'   -TOOLu- 'be married'
         -TOOLįsį- 'arrange marriage of'
         umuTOOLį/iaTOOLį 'bridegroom(s)'
         umuTOOLua/iaTOOLua 'bride(s)'
         uuTOOLį 'marriage'

BEMBA: -UP- 'marry'   -UPu- 'be married'
         -UFi- 'arrange marriage of'
         iciUPo 'marriage'   ubuUFi 'married state'

MBUNDU: -KUel- 'marry'   -KUelis- 'arrange marriage of'
         -KUeliu- 'be married'
         oloHUela 'marriage'

The main thing to note from these examples is that either of the consonants of the radical may be variable within the one group of words built from it. Thus in BEMBA the final consonant is sometimes **-P-** and sometimes **-F-**, while in MBUNDU the radical given has **-K-** or **-H-** as its first consonant.

The example from FAŊ demonstrates that though the subsidiary criteria may be difficult to apply, they are not entirely inapplicable in a language of this kind. In such cases it is usually possible to determine the radical, but the large number of words without a suffix often creates problems in the distinguishing of verbals from nominals.

Similarly it is frequently difficult to identify the extensions and to distinguish them from suffixes, as may be seen in the above example.

The importance of the criterion of the invariability of the stem of nominals in two-class genders can best be illustrated in a negative way. There is an obscure language called Ndabe spoken near the Bantu frontier in the Cameroons. It has some features which resemble those usually laid down for Bantu languages, but many of its words behave like these:

nyu/nyol 'knee(s)'   **mfo(‿)/mfo (⁻)** 'slave(s)'
fo/fal 'head(s)'   **ke(‿)/ke (⁻)** 'finger(s)'

Thus in spite of the fact that there is a kind of grammatical agreement between these words and the numerals, the language cannot be accepted as Bantu.

Some difficulty may arise with respect to the criterion that only verbals used as interjections are entirely without prefix. This occurs in a number of languages of Zone A which have zero prefix in some cases. Thus in DUMA (A.72), for example, the personal prefixes in the plural are **lį-** for the first and second persons and **ba-** for the third person. In the singular, however, all three persons have zero prefix, which might be mistaken for a case of a word with no prefix at all: e.g. **mwana yimba** 'the child is singing'.

Up to the present no language accepted as Bantu has been found in which verbals in simple sentences are always without a prefix, and indeed this would appear to be completely foreign to Bantu structure. In those languages where it might be argued that the sign of agreement with its subject is a self-standing 'pronoun', there is an increasing tendency always to use this, in such a way that it is debatable whether or not it should be separated from the verbal. For example, in BASA (A.44) **me pam** or **mepam** 'I arrived'.

4. The Balanced Radical Vowel System

To illustrate the Bantu vowel system here are two complete series of radicals, one from a seven-vowel language and one from a five-vowel language. The tonal behaviour of the radicals is identical throughout, and no other radicals exist with these consonants and this tonal behaviour.

BUBAŊGĮ (C.21b): -BAL- 'count', -BĮL- 'follow', -BIL- 'border', -BEL- 'be annoyed', -BŲL- 'be numerous', -BUL- 'break', -BOL- 'rot'.

BEMBA (M.42a): -LAL- 'crack', -LIL- 'cry', -LEL- 'rear', -LUL- 'become bitter', -LOL- 'have the eyes open'.

What was said about MFINU in the paragraph on the related vocabulary will be sufficient to show how it may be practically impossible to apply this criterion to such languages.

Languages which are incompletely Bantu

As might have been expected, there are languages in which some of the criteria we have established hold good, but some do not. An example of one kind of such a partly Bantu language is seen in *BĮRA* (D.32). In this language the vocabulary relationship referred to in the second criterion is quite clear, as also the structural features and vowel system of the third and fourth criteria. The grammatical agreement and gender system, however, is distinctly fragmentary. There is, for example, only one type of prefix alternation between singular and plural nominals, **mbuhu/babuhu** 'person(s)', **ŋkama/bakama** 'chief(s)'. The greater part of the nominals are invariable, although the element **ba-** may be prefixed as a sign of the plural, e.g. **kịma/bakịma** 'thing(s)', **kịboko** 'arm(s)', **ganị** 'word(s)'. The system of agreement by means of dependent prefixes is equally incomplete. Words like **mbuhu** govern agreements of this kind, **mindo maŋkina** 'this other', while those like **babuhu** govern these agreements, **bendo baŋkina** 'these others'. The remainder of the words, however, govern the same kind of agreement, whether they are singular or plural, and whether they have the prefix **ba-** or not: e.g. **kịma lake lando maŋkina** 'this other thing of his', **bakịma lake lando maŋkina** 'these other things of his'. There are only two verbal prefixes, **a-** which is usually singular, and **ba-** which is usually plural.

Although languages of this kind cannot be called Bantu owing to their not having the complete prefix system we have described as a criterion, their relationship to the Bantu languages is sufficiently close for them to be taken into account. We shall therefore call them 'Sub-Bantu'. Some of the lingua franca languages like *MAŊGALA* (C.26d) are in this category, since they have well-defined two-class genders, like the true Bantu languages, but little or no prefix agreement in dependent words.

A second type of language which obeys only some of the criteria is found in the Cameroons and south-eastern Nigeria. These languages obey the first criterion but not the others. That means that while they have a system of grammatical genders and agreements operated by means of prefixes, they show little or no relationship of vocabulary with full Bantu languages. In addition they do not display even the rudiments of the structural features laid down in the third criterion; moreover their vowel system is frequently complicated. An example of this may be seen in BAFUT, a language spoken in the British Cameroons near the Bantu frontier. There are such genders as **muŋwị/buŋwị** 'knife(s)', **azo/njo** 'thing(s)', **ati/üti** 'tree(s)'. There are such agreements as **muŋwị kụla** 'this knife', **buŋwị bụla** 'these knives', **nülịhị nụla** 'this eye', **mịhị mụla** 'these eyes', **ŋụ gụla** 'this man', **bö bụla** 'these men'. This kind of grammatical behaviour is definitely reminiscent of what happens in the languages we have accepted as Bantu, but it cannot be used to establish any clear relationship such as exists in the case of the Sub-Bantu languages. We shall therefore adopt the term 'Bantoid' to describe any language that has a system of prefix genders and agreements of this kind without any other Bantu features.

In view of the great difference between these two kinds of partially Bantu languages, it is natural to treat them differently. The Bantoid languages are therefore not dealt with at all in this work, but the Sub-Bantu languages are placed within the scheme of classification, being distinguished by the use of italic type.

CHAPTER III
METHODS OF CLASSIFICATION

WE now have to consider the answers to the question, 'How are the Bantu languages to be classified?' For our present purpose we may ignore the method used by Cust, which has little or no linguistic basis, being merely geographical. There are, however, other systems of classification which are based on linguistic facts. These may be roughly divided into three types: (1) The Historical, (2) The Empirical, (3) The Practical. We shall take each of these in turn.

1. THE HISTORICAL METHOD

It was Meinhof who advocated this method of classification, principally as an outcome of the technique of comparative Bantu phililogy he originated. Briefly it would involve the establishing of a genealogical table for the language family. From this it would then be possible to assert that the members of a given group had sprung from a common ancestor, which was itself a late descendant of the common parent of all Bantu.

There is no need for us to discuss here the implications or the merits of this technique, since the likelihood of its being able to produce results is so remote. Some useful deductions may be made about the sounds of the hypothetical common Bantu, but in a field with practically no historical records, true historical study, as distinct from comparative study, is impossible.

From what Meinhof himself says in the chapter on classification in his *Introduction to the Phonology of the Bantu Languages*, one may suspect that he realized the nature of the problem involved in the technique he advocates. In fact this is the least convincing chapter in the whole work.

2. THE EMPIRICAL METHOD

The essence of this method consists in the drawing of isoglosses on the map in order to show the distribution of various linguistic features. Then if several of the isoglosses coincide, this may be taken as the boundary between different language areas. In practice, however, it means that certain differentia are chosen, and then used in an attempt to divide up the area covered by the Bantu languages. Since this method is the one that has been implied in most of the classifications made so far, it must be considered in some detail, both as to its implications and as to its results.

First then as to the method itself. What are the linguistic differentia that can be used for plotting isoglosses? The following list includes every type that may be so used.

(a) Lexical, i.e. as to differences of vocabulary.
(b) Grammatical, i.e. as to differences of form and sentence structure.
(c) Phonological, i.e. as to differences of distinction between sound units.
(d) Phonetic, i.e. as to differences in the actual sounds of speech.
(e) Tonal, i.e. as to differences in the tone system.

We must then study each of these types of differentia, and try to show what results can be achieved by their use.

(a) *Lexical Differentia*

There are two kinds of lexical differentia. One is concerned with the distribution of actual words and the other with the distinctive features of the words in the vocabulary.

The first of these kinds was used chiefly by Johnstone, who has shown that some very interesting results can be achieved by means of it. If, for example, we plot the occurrence of these five words for 'house', *NYUMBA, *NGANDA, *NJUBU, *NDAGU, *NJO, we get well-defined areas. Unfortunately, however, as had already been pointed out by Meinhof, isoglosses obtained in this way from one set of words rarely coincide with those obtained from another set. Instead of plotting the areas where the different words for one idea occur, it is also possible to plot the limits of the distribution of certain widely occurring words which can all be related to one common starred form. Thus, for example, the isoglosses for the occurrence of *-LEET- 'bring', *-LEK- 'leave', *-LIM- 'cultivate', *-TUUL- 'put down', *-PU̧AL- 'wear', *-BI̧AL- 'give birth to', *MULI̧ 'village', all show a remarkable similarity in that none of these roots is represented in the languages north-west of a line from Benguella through Léopoldville to Stanleyville. Experiment proves that this second method of plotting isoglosses is much more useful than the first.

One of the difficulties in any system of classification based merely on words is that there is rarely a sudden break in the distribution of vocabulary, apart from occasional cases like the one just given in the previous paragraph. A study of the fragmentary word-lists given by Johnstone shows that adjacent languages frequently have vocabularies that are similar, and it was this fact that led him to base his classification largely on words. It is also an unfortunate fact that all too often the sum total of our knowledge of a language is contained in a list of words, and this frequently of doubtful reliability. The important thing for our present purpose, however, is that any system of classification based on words has an essential weakness. This inheres in the fact that vocabulary can so easily be borrowed by one language from another without effectively bringing the two languages closer together.

There is only one satisfactory way in which the closeness of the relationship between languages can be determined by means of word-lists. This involves the application of the technique of comparative study based on the use of hypothetical starred forms. Briefly it consists in the compilation for each language of a 'standard' vocabulary of about a thousand distinct words of common occurrence. That the words should be distinct simply means the avoidance of duplication, thus if **-lul-** 'become bitter' and **-lulu** 'bitter' both occur in a language, only one of them may be put into the standard vocabulary.

When such vocabularies have been made for many languages, it will usually be found that just over three hundred of the words in a given language, i.e. about 30 per cent., can be related to corresponding words in at least two other languages by means of the comparative method, by which starred forms may thus be established.

Taking then one such standard vocabulary, and comparing it with that of another language spoken at a considerable distance, we shall usually find that the proportion of the vocabulary common to the two falls far below the 30 per cent. By taking other languages at distances becoming progressively less, we sometimes find that along a certain line there is a sudden jump in the percentage of related words. This line may then be taken as part of an isogloss. The important feature of this method is the insistence on fixed rules of relationship to the starred forms in all cases, since this reduces the likelihood of misleading figures due to loan-words.

Lexical differentia of the second kind, which have scarcely been considered at all up to this time, consist mainly of features which have a phonological or tonal significance. The isoglosses provided by these features give much more interesting results than those obtained by plotting individual words. Since, however, we shall be studying characteristics of this kind in sections (c) and (e), it will be preferable to leave them till then. There are a few other minor features which can be used, such as the following.

(i) The existence or not of any partial correlation of certain genders with notions of relative size. For example, in LUBA-LULUA (L.31) there is a gender **ka/tu** which contains such words as **kasoko/tusoko** 'small village(s)' related to **musoko/misoko** 'village(s)', even though a large number of words in this gender have no reference to small things, e.g., **kapia/tupia** 'fire(s)'. In BUBAŊGI (C.21b), on the other hand, there is nothing corresponding to this.

(ii) The existence or not of regular types of nominals related to the radicals of verbals. For example, in KOŊGO (H.16f) there are many kinds of nominals related to **-sumb-** 'buy', including **nsumbi/basumbi** 'purchaser(s)', **nsumba** 'manner of purchasing', **nsumbo/nsumbo** 'act(s) of buying'. MFINU (B.41), on the other hand, has no related nominals of this kind.

(b) Grammatical Differentia

These are some of the most useful differentia for classification, but the only writer who has made any serious use of them is Doke, and even he introduces them in a subsidiary way. There are naturally many things that could be included under this heading and it is found that the isoglosses given by the more important of these frequently tend to coincide. Here are some of them, including those which could not have been used previously through lack of data.

(i) The existence or not of double nominal prefixes. For example, BEMBA (M.42a) has **umuntu** 'person', while LENJE (M.61) has **muntu** 'person'.

(ii) The existence or not of the extra independent prefixes *PA-, *KU-, *MU-. For example, LUBA-LULUA (L.31) has **panzubu** 'on the house', **kunzubu** 'towards the house', and **munzubu** 'in the house', while TETELA (C.71) to the immediate north-west has nothing corresponding to this type of grammatical form.

(iii) The existence or not of nasal consonants in the dependent prefixes. For example, in KOŊGO (H.16f) there is **ntima mieto** 'our hearts', but in NDOŊGO (H.21) **miṣima ietu** 'our hearts'.

(iv) The method, if any, of modifying the prefix of a nominal when it is used as a sentence. For example, in each of the three following languages 'oil' is **amafuta**, but 'it is oil' in NYIHA (M.23) is **mafuta**, in TOTELA (K.41) **maafuta**, and in HA (D.66) **nimafuta**.

(v) The use or not of the suffix *-E in dependent tenses. For example, 'let us send' in MOŊGO-ŊKUNDU (C.61) is **tutume**, but in BUBAŊGI (C.21b) it is **tutuma**.

(vi) The use or not of suffixes other than *-A in principal affirmative tenses. For example, KIKUYU (E.51) has -įre and -iite, whereas WUNJO (E.62b) has nothing but -a.

(vii) The system of tense signs. These vary enormously over the whole Bantu field, but similar features may be found within a group. For example, in Group E.30 there is the unusual tense sign *-AKA- -E used to refer to events in the immediate future.

(viii) The structure of negative statements. There are certain well-defined types of formal negatives in Bantu languages; for example, BUBADGĮ (C.21b) uses an independent negative particle at the end of the sentence, while ŊGOMBE (C.31) has special negative tenses containing negative elements.

(ix) The use or not of infixes as substitute objects of verbals. For example, 'he fears me' in TIO (B.35) is **abara me,** but in MFINU (B.41) **ambara**.

(x) The method of constructing relative clauses. There are several of these; for example, in SUKUMA (F.21) we find **kinhu ikiaġua** 'the thing which has fallen', but in GOGO (G.11) **icinhu ciono ciaġua** 'the thing which has fallen'.

(c) *Phonological Differentia*

Features of this kind have not previously been used for purposes of classification. They are, however, very useful and produce some interesting isoglosses. The definition of this type of differentia as given above was: 'differences in the distinctions between sound units'. Since, however, the term 'phonology' has been used in more than one sense, it is perhaps important to illustrate fairly fully the characteristics to which it refers here.

The phonological differentia are not concerned with the actual sounds used in speech, nor with the deduced 'sound-changes' studied in comparative Bantu philology. For example, in Swahili **-keŋg-** 'deceive' and **-ceŋg-** 'lop' are different radicals, whereas in Bemba **-ceŋg-** 'treat unfairly' is not distinguished from **-keŋg-**. At this point we are not interested in the fact that the **-c-** in the Swahili radicals corresponds to an **-s-** in Bemba (as Swahili **-cek-** and Bemba **-sek-** 'laugh') since that belongs to comparative study. Neither does it matter whether the **-c-** of Swahili is identical in pronunciation with the **-c-** of Bemba, since that is a phonetic question. Phonologically the significant thing is that there is an alternance c/k before **-e-** in the first consonant of the radical in Swahili but not in Bemba.

Another illustration of this kind of characteristic may be seen in the occurrence of an alternance l/r. In TIO (B.35) **-kal-** 'dwell' must be distinguished from **-kar-** 'be tied', whereas in KOŊGO (H.16f) **-kal-** 'dwell' is not distinct from **-kar-**. This means that there is an alternance l/r in the second consonant of the radical in Tio but not in Koŋgo.

Similarly in NYANJA (N.31a) there is an alternance l/d in the first consonant of the radical, but in YAO (P.21) there is not. For example, in Nyanja **-lul-** 'froth up' has to be distinguished from **-dul-** 'cut off', but in Yao **-lul-** 'froth up' is not distinct from **-dul-**.

Apart from the alternances in the consonants of the radical, which are too numerous to list, there are also other types of phonological differentia. Of the selection given in the following list some relate to alternances in the sounds of lexical elements, and others to those of grammatical elements, but it is simplest to deal with them all under this heading.

(i) The existence or not of alternations i/į and u/ų in the radical vowel. This could be expressed differently as an alternance of seven as against one of five vowel sounds in the radical. For example, RUIHI (P.12) distinguishes between the vowels in the radicals -įmb- 'swell' and -imb- 'sing', whereas YAO (P.21) -imb- 'swell' is not distinct from -įmb-.

(ii) The existence or not of an alternance of vowel quantity in the radical. For example, BEMBA (M.42a) distinguishes the vowel in -fum- 'go out' from that in -fuum- 'drizzle', but MWAŊGA (M.22) does not distinguish -fum- 'go out' from -fuum-.

(iii) The existence or not of alternations i/e and u/o in suffixes. For example, in KIKUYU (E.51) ndįhu 'spray' has to be distinguished from ndįho 'big club', whereas in BUBAŊGI (C.21b) ŋkįŋgu 'neck' is not distinct from ŋkįŋgo.

(iv) Whether or not the alternations in the consonants of the extensions are similar to those in the consonants of the radicals. For example, the alternance s/z occurs in the first consonant of the radical in both GANDA (E.15a) and KOŊGO (H.16f), since Ganda distinguishes -sin- 'nauseate' from -zin- 'dance', and Koŋgo distinguishes -sin- 'be deep' from -zin- 'be burnt'. On the other hand, Ganda has a similar alternance in extensions, while Koŋgo has not; thus in Ganda -lamus- 'greet' has to be distinguished from -lamuz- 'bargain with', 'whereas in Koŋgo -sekes- 'whet' is not distinct from -sekez-.

(v) Whether or not there are alternations in the vowels of extensions similar to those of the radical and those of the suffix. For example, LUNDA (L.52), which has the alternations i/e and u/o in radicals but not in suffixes, has similar alternations in extensions. Thus though **mukonu** 'leg' is not distinct from **mukono, -saluk-** 'come out in a rash' must be distinguished from **-salok-** 'be restless in sleep'. Other languages like LUBA-LULUA (L.31) have no such alternance in the extensions.

(vi) Whether or not there is a similar alternance of quantity in the vowels of the extensions and those of the radicals. For example, both BEMBA (M.42a) and KOŊGO (H.16f) have an alternance of quantity in radicals, since Bemba distinguishes -kul- 'grow up' from -kuul- 'extract' and Koŋgo distinguishes -kul- 'grow up' from -kuul- 'liberate'. In extensions, however, Bemba has a similar alternance of quantity, whereas Koŋgo does not; thus -pelel- 'sow broadcast' in Bemba is distinct from -peleel- 'almost arrive', but in Koŋgo -kelel- 'filter for' is not distinguished from -keleel-.

(d) Phonetic Differentia

Characteristics of this kind have been used more than once in attempts at classification, but these attempts have frequently failed through the inaccuracies in the available phonetic data. Moreover, data of this kind are not of much value in certain cases since similar phonetic processes are to be found in many languages outside the Bantu family. Thus, for example, the fact that the syllables *KI and *KE are pronounced **ci** and **ce** in the languages of Group M.50 means little, as the same rules holds good in some European languages, such as Italian.

Here, however, are a few phonetic features which occasionally produce some useful isoglosses.

(i) The existence or not of vowel length at an internal vowel junction, or before a nasal compound. For example, neither LENJE (M.61) nor NYANJA (N.31a) has an alternance of quantity in the vowel of the radical, but whereas in Lenje **muana** 'child' is pronounced **mwaana** (when it is the subject of the sentence), in Nyanja a similar word is pronounced **mwana**.

(ii) The existence or not of phonetic prominence on certain syllables, such as radical intensity, or penultimate vowel length. For example, in BUBAŊGI̧ (C.21b) the two following words both have radical intensity, which means that in the first the prominence is on the first syllable, and in the second on the second, **LOKolo**! 'emulate!' and **loKOLo** 'cock's comb'. In BEMBA (M.42a), on the other hand, the pronunciation of the two following words is identical, showing that there is no radical prominence, **ukuFISulula** 'to bring out of hiding', **ukufiSULula** 'to invert them (i.e. things)'.

(iii) The behaviour of junctions involving a nasal consonant. There are many different types of such behaviour, including even a reduction of the number of alternances represented in the pronunciation. For example, YAO (P.21) has identical pronunciation of **nTEKe** 'let me draw (water)' and **nLEKe** 'let me leave', both being heard as **ndeke**, while in BEMBA (M.42a) there is nothing like this. In Bemba, on the other hand, the first syllable in each of the two following words is pronounced identically as **nno-**, **nNOŊKe** 'let me acquire', **nLOŊGe** 'let me pack', whereas in KOŊGO (H.16f) this would not happen.

(iv) The behaviour of double vowel junctions. For example, in NYARUANDA (D.61) **ubuato** 'canoe' is heard as **ubgato**, while in ZIBA (E.22a) a similar word, **ubuato**, is heard as **ubwaato**.

(v) The behaviour of the consonant **k-** in the syllable preceding a radical commencing with a voiceless consonant. For example, in HA (D.66) the first consonant in **kulima** 'to hoe' is heard as **k-**, while the first in **kutema** 'to cut' is heard as **g-**, but in HOROHORO (D.28) the first consonant of the similar words **kulima** and **kutema** is heard as **k-** in both cases.

(e) Tonal Differentia

Some very useful isoglosses are provided by differentia of this kind, though nobody has previously used them, since there has been inadequate information on the subject. There are, however, two main types of these differentia, one as to the tonal alternances, and one as to the relation between these alternances and the actual tones of speech.

Within the compass of this present work it is manifestly impossible to deal in detail with these interesting questions. One result of this is that the following features merely indicate some of the observed facts without any explanation as to how they were obtained. Moreover, this list of tonal differentia by no means includes all those which I have so far been able to establish.

(i) The existence or not of an alternance of tone on the radical. For example, in BENA (G.64) there are two kinds of tonal behaviour for radicals of a given shape,

-gul- 'buy' and -let- 'bring' being typical of these. In GOGO (G.11), on the other hand, there is only one kind of tonal behaviour for all radicals of a given shape, and the corresponding radicals -gul- and -let- always have identical tone-patterns.

(ii) The existence or not of an alternance of tone on the nominal suffix. For example, in BUBAḌGỊ (C.21b) nominals with a dissyllabic stem fall into four tone-groups, which may be represented by these type words, **mbịndu** 'dirt', **ŋgandu** 'crocodile', **mpamba** 'nothing', **nduŋgu** 'pepper', whereas in KOḌGO (H.16f) all such words fall into two tone-groups only.

(iii) The existence or not of an alternance of tone on extensions in nominals. For example, in BUBAḌGỊ (C.21b) there is a difference in the tone-patterns of these two words, **mukililị** (_ _ _ _) 'agent', and **muliŋgilị** (_ _ ¯ _) 'calmness', whereas in VENḌA (S.11) a difference of this kind does not exist.

(iv) The existence or not of a tonal alternance in dependent prefixes. There are several types of such alternances, so it is only possible here to select one as an illustration. In SUKUMA (F.21) the tone-pattern of the verbal is different in the two following cases, **burị ikufụma** (_ _ _ _ _ _) 'the goat will go out', **burị ịịkufụma** (_ _ _ ¯ _ _) 'the goats will go out'. In HA (D.66), however, there is no difference in the tone-pattern of the corresponding verbals.

(v) The use or not of tone-patterns determined by the syntactical relationships of words. For example, in MFINU (B.41) the tone-pattern of the first word is different in the two following cases, **leburu lemo** (_ ¯ _ ¯ _) 'one tribe', **leburu leso** (_ _ _ ¯ ¯ _) 'that tribe', whereas in TIO (B.35) a similar word **libura** 'tribe' has only one tone-pattern whatever its context.

The Results of Applying the Differentia

From the list of differentia just given it might be thought that if these were used for plotting isoglosses, the classification of the Bantu languages would be a simple matter. Unfortunately, however, this is far from what is found when the attempt is made. A number of the differentia in the list were described as 'useful' and this is by no means incorrect. The real difficulty lies in the fact that none of the differentia can be applied consistently over the whole of the Bantu field. This is not through lack of data, nor is it because the differentia may sometimes be inapplicable, as, for example, when languages like BUBAḌGỊ (C.21b) do not use nominals as sentences and so the one in section *b* (v) cannot be applied. What actually happens is that each of the characteristics gives good results in at least one area but not in another.

If the empirical method of classification is to be used consistently each of the differentia should be equally valid wherever applied, otherwise the method collapses. An example or two will make clear the impossibility of the regular application of this method. The extreme case of its failure occurs when an isogloss provided by a given feature coincides with others in indicating a useful division between languages in one part of the field and then cuts right through the middle of a single language elsewhere. For example, the use of prefix **ku-** in place of the prefix **tu-** for the first person plural agrees with several other differentia in dividing the languages of Group E.30 from those of Group E.10. When we try to apply the same distinction farther south, however, we find that it marks a boundary right through the middle of NYAMWESỊ

(F.22) where **ku-** is used in the south and **tu-** in the north, but in this case the isogloss is solitary, and so cannot be used.

Similarly the existence of a seven-vowel system in radicals usually distinguishes a language from a neighbouring one with a five-vowel system in such a way that the languages are found to belong to different groups, e.g. Group C.20 has seven vowels, but B.30 and B.40 five, F.20 has seven and E.20 five, S.20 has seven and S.30 five. Yet the isogloss arising from this difference is almost the only one separating NYIHA (M.23) from MALILA (M.24).

Our conclusion on the empirical method then is that it cannot be used without some modification, and this question will be discussed in the next section.

3. The Practical Method

The present work follows a practical system of classification. This means that the presence of some arbitrariness is admitted as an essential modification of the empirical method. It is presumably because others have not made this admission that no satisfactory classification has yet been achieved. Let us at this point then see exactly what we are trying to do.

The relationships of the languages we accept as Bantu by applying our criteria are sufficiently clear to make some classification possible, while the number of the languages found in this family makes classification almost essential. There are two ways in which this can be undertaken. We may begin with the whole field and try to put in some boundaries to divide it up into a number of large sections. Then by a process of sub-division we may go on until we reach the smallest useful unit. This classification by fragmentation has been the technique adopted by almost all those who have previously attempted to classify the Bantu languages. There is, however, a quite different approach which may be used. Suppose we take the individual language as our starting-point, and then move outwards from it. It is possible in this way to group together with the language from which we started other adjacent languages which display similar characteristics. At some point we shall decide that we have moved into another group. The decision will, however, have an element of arbitrariness in it, because although we shall be able to assert that the group displays a certain set of common characteristics, the distribution of any of these may not be coextensive with the group. The arbitrariness lies in the exact set of characteristics we choose. If a more restricted set were chosen the group would be larger, and conversely if a wider set were chosen the group would be smaller. Moreover, it may sometimes happen that although a given set of characteristics is displayed by a group, in one member the most important of these is missing, yet in all other respects it is clearly necessary that it should be included in the group.

In the classification described in the next chapter it is this second technique which I have followed. This means that the whole of the Bantu field is shown as consisting of a number of groups of varying size and closeness of relationship. Since there are nearly eighty of these groups, some larger unit is clearly necessary for ease of reference. To place the groups in sets, a similar method is employed in which an arbitrary blend of characteristics is made. Naturally the validity of these larger units is less than that of the groups, but still the prevailing consideration in the establishing of such sets is linguistic. It proves convenient to make sixteen of these sets, which are called zones.

By zone, therefore, is to be understood primarily a set of groups which have a certain geographical contiguity and which display a number of common linguistic features as well.

The use of the term 'arbitrary' must not lead the reader to think that the classification is capricious. As already stated, the arbitrariness consists in the choice of the differentia to be used in each case, and not in dispensing with the use of differentia. Thus, for example, at the meeting of the three Zones B, C, and H there is a bunching of so many isoglosses that any system of classification would have to place important boundaries here. But the net result of this practical system is simply that in citing the characteristics of any group or zone we can only state them broadly, and that in actual fact there will usually be some important exceptions. This, however, can hardly be held to be a defect of the system, but rather an inevitable outcome of the facts. We are faced with a situation in which we either have to introduce some element of arbitrariness or give up all attempts at classification.

What is claimed for the present work is that by taking into account as many features as possible the arbitrariness is reduced to a minimum. Moreover, since it is avowedly practical in its intention, similarities between widely separated languages are of little importance, and we shall avoid the kind of grouping suggested by Torrend and Jacottet which places together SUTHU (S.23), MAKUA (P.31), and MPUDGWE (A.71a).

CHAPTER IV

THE BANTU LANGUAGES CLASSIFIED

It now remains simply to set out some of the results achieved by the application of the practical method just outlined. Before we do so, however, something must be said about the use of the terms 'language' and 'dialect'.

Here again we are faced with a situation in which no clear decision can be reached on purely scientific grounds. Moreover, there are added difficulties arising both from political considerations and from demographic data. Thus from a purely linguistic point of view there is no real reason for treating ZULU (S.32) as distinct from Xhosa (S.31), they could easily be regarded as a cluster of dialects. Yet to do so would mean ignoring the fact that the speakers of these two forms of speech have come to regard themselves as speaking two different languages. Similarly there might be some justification for treating SUKUMA (F.21) and NYAMWESI (F.22) as a dialect cluster, but it happens that the speakers of Sukuma are far more numerous than those of Nyamwesi, and that for political and demographic reasons we have to consider them as separate languages. Thus in deciding what is to be regarded as a distinct language, and what as a mere dialect, not only have we no watertight linguistic test to apply, but we have to bring in other considerations which are entirely non-linguistic.

In this way it is quite likely that the part of the following classification which will need most revision is that relating to the distinction between languages and dialects. In some cases the test of inter-intelligibility may be applied, but even this cannot be used without arbitrariness since one has first to decide the nature of the topics to be dealt with in such a test. Thus it may easily happen that a speaker of one language finds no difficulty in conversing with the speaker of another when they confine themselves to simple trading affairs, but yet these same two would be quite unable to understand each other in a discussion of some point of difference in their social customs.

NUMERATION

As mentioned in the introductory chapter the method of numbering the languages has been presupposed by the use of the references whenever a language has been mentioned in the preceding chapters. The system worked out enables any language to be referred to by a letter and two figures. Each group is indicated by a figure, and the number of the language within the group by a second figure. Thus 42 means the second language in the fourth group. When the group as a whole is referred to, zero is used in place of the second figure, so 40 means the fourth group in a given zone.

Where there is a dialect cluster, this also is given a number like the single languages, and then the individual dialects are distinguished by additional small letters. For example, MYENE (A.71) is a cluster of three dialects, MPUDGWE (A.71a), Ruŋgu (A.71b), and GALWA (A.71c).

There are sixteen zones in all, so that it would not have been practicable to use a purely geographical method of referring to them. Instead, each zone has been given a letter, and this is put immediately before the figures denoting the language in each case. Thus to say that BEMBA is M.42 means that it is the second language in the fourth group of Zone M, and consequently is in some measure related to a language like FIPA (M.13).

AUTHORITIES

In a work of this size it is not practicable to cite all the authorities for the data used. As has been stated in the first chapter, much of the information has been gathered at first hand, but there are still some very large gaps in our knowledge of the Bantu field. It is clearly desirable to show where such gaps exist, so some of the languages are given an initial capital only, but others are put entirely in the upper case. It is only with respect to the latter that there are sufficient data to make the classification reasonably reliable. This is not to say that all the data used are equally trustworthy, or that the grouping is in any way authoritative, but simply to indicate that in such cases it is at least based on something beyond mere word-lists.

Where a language is referred to by a name written with an initial capital only, nothing is known, apart from what may be given in Johnstone's work, beyond the probability that there is such a language. When dealing with languages like these, one of two very unsatisfactory expedients has had to be adopted. Either the languages have been grouped on the basis of the meagre information contained in the word-lists, or a relationship asserted by some earlier writer has perforce been used. It will therefore be very likely that when more data become available a considerable modification of the classification may be necessary in such cases. It does not seem probable, however, that it will be necessary to make any more groups, but rather a reassortment of the languages between the groups. The numeration of the well-known languages will therefore be able to stand, and in this way we are provided, for those languages with some documentation, with a means of simple reference which can be used in general Bantu language studies or in the cataloguing of linguistic works.

CLASSIFIED LIST

Since the map only bears the reference numbers of the languages, it was necessary to provide a key to it in the form of a complete classified list. For this reason no full list is given at this point, but instead the groups in each zone are set out as the zones are studied in turn.

As was shown in the preceding chapter, the zones are not made on purely linguistic grounds. This means that in some cases the groups placed in one zone display a much closer linguistic relationship than those placed in others. Clearly the only satisfactory development of the technique adopted would have been a description of the linguistic characteristics of each of the groups. That, however, would have been far beyond the scope of this monograph. Instead, therefore, the zones are described in some detail, which throws into relief the nature of the relationship between the groups in any given zone.

In some cases the features noted are divided into two sets. There are what are termed 'common features', which are the ones not common to the whole of the Bantu field but nevertheless to be found to some extent in adjacent zones. Then there are the 'peculiar features', which are not necessarily confined exclusively to the zone in question, but which do not appear to occur in any of the languages immediately adjoining it.

ZONE A

GROUP 10	GROUP 40	GROUP 60
11 Ŋgolo	41 Bati	61 YAUNDE
12 KUNDU	42 BO	62 BULU
13 Mboŋge	43 Koko	63 Ntum
14 Lue	44 BASA	64 Maka
15 LUNDU	45 Sịkị	65 Zịmu
	46 ŊGUMBA	66 FAŊ
	47 Gbea	67 Make

GROUP 20		
21 Mbuku		
22 KWIRỊ	GROUP 50	GROUP 70
23 SUBU	51 NOHU	71 MYENE
24 DỤALA	52 Naka	71a MPUŊGWE
	53 Laŋgị	71b Ruŋgu
	54 Ŋgumbi	71c GALWA
	55 BEŊGA	72 DỤMA
GROUP 30		73 KELE
31 BUBI	56 Seke	74 KUTA

Characteristics of the Zone

In this zone there is considerable linguistic relationship between the different groups, and it proves possible to list in some detail the features which characterize it.

I. *Common Features*

1. The absence of any genders regularly containing words which indicate smallness or bigness. (Also in Zones B and C.)

2. The absence of an extension **-u-**. There are passive verbals of one kind or another in a number of the languages of this zone, but only in BEŊGA (55) has anything been noted which even resembles the -u- of other zones. For example, **uluma** 'to send', **ulumakue** 'to be sent'. (Also in Zones B and C.)

3. The use of single independent nominal prefixes only. (Also in Zones B and C.)

4. The use of particles rather than extra independent prefixes. For example, in BỤBI (31) **u-ite** 'at the stone', **a-ite** 'to the stone', or in KELE (73) **pe-dịkokị** 'on the stone'. An interesting isolated exception occurs in Group 10, where LUNDU (15) has an extra prefix **u-**, as in **undabu** 'in the house', which can govern an agreement, e.g. **undabu ubukị** 'in the house it is bad'. (Also in Zone C.)

5. The use of nominals as sentences without any prefix modification. For example, in MYENE (71) **aramba** 'roots', **mano aramba** 'those are roots', or in LUNDU (15) **bikaka binene** 'big mats' or 'the mats are big ones'. (Also in Zones B and C.)

6 The occurrence of dependent tenses without the suffix ***-E**. This is by no means without exception, even within one group, e.g. MPUŊGWE (71a) **-gend-** 'go', **wịkagende** '(that) they should go', KELE (72) **-lum-** 'send', **balumịkị** '(that) they should send', KUTA (74) **-pik-** 'do', **bapikakye** '(that) they may do'. Apart from the two examples just given, the suffix **-e** in dependent tenses only appears to occur in Groups 10 and 20. (Also in Zones B and C.)

7. The absence of the verbal suffix *-ILE which occurs in many other zones. (Also in Zones B and C.)

8. The rarity of true negative tenses. FAD (66) and MYENE (71) apparently use a difference of tone-pattern as the sole sign of the negative in some tenses. In other languages the negative element is simply added to affirmative sentences, either to the verbal as affix, or elsewhere in the sentence. For example, in LUNDU (15) there is the infix -sa-, **nalaŋgaka** 'I am reading', **nasalaŋgaka** 'I am not reading', and in DUALA (24) the -si-, **nalumi** 'I sent', **nasilumi** 'I did not send'. In BASA (44), on the other hand, there is a self-standing negative word **bi** at the end of the negative clause, e.g. **agatimp bi** 'he will not return', cf. **agatimp** 'he will return'; and in DUMA (72) there is a double sign **ka . . . ve**, e.g. **bisu livovi** 'we have spoken', **bisu kalivovi ve** 'we have not spoken'. The principal exceptions to this are in BEDGA (55), where the negative of **hukabapandi** 'we shall carry' is the shorter word **huabapa**, and in KELE (73), where the negative of **meelaŋ** 'I will count' is the distinct tense **mecilaŋ**. (Also in Zones B and C.)

9. The substitute object rarely an infix, but usually a self-standing word. For example, in LUNDU (15) **bauki si** 'they have heard us'. The principal exception to this is in BUBI (31), e.g. **tutapi** 'we have shown', **tubutapi** 'we have shown him'. (Also in Zone B.)

10. The absence of an alternance k/g in radicals except as the first radical consonant preceded by a nasal consonant. For example, in FAD (66) **ilak** 'to say' but **lage** 'say!' (there are no non-fricative velar consonants in this position in this language), cf. **ŋkum** 'bellows', **ŋgum** 'hedgehog'; or in MPUDGWE (71a) **ikamba** 'to speak', but **gamba** 'speak!', cf. **ŋkola** 'shell', **ŋgola** 'whirlpool'. (Also in Zones B and C.)

11. A seven-vowel system which appears to be characteristic of the whole zone. (Also Zone C.)

12. A single quantity only in radical vowels. (Also in Zones B and C.)

II. *Peculiar Features*

1. The small percentage of words in the standard vocabularies which can be related to those in languages of other zones. For example, in MYENE (71) and KELE (73) there are only 8 per cent. and in FAD (66) only 5 per cent. On the other hand, although FAD is not very closely related in other ways to the languages of Group 70, it has an additional 20 per cent. of words which can be related to the standard vocabularies of that group.

2. Unusual types of relationship between extended radicals and simple radicals. For example, in BO (42) there are these typical series of radicals, **-kag-** 'bind', **-kegi-** 'get bound', **-keges-** 'cause to bind'; **-bom-** 'hit', **-bumi-** 'get hit', **-buma-** 'be hit (by)'.

3. The existence of two different classes of nominals with distinct independent prefixes and governing different dependent prefixes, but both having their plural in the class with the prefix **ba-**. For example, in BEDGA (55) **ukali mune** 'this speaker', pl. **bakali bane**; **mutu mone** 'this person', pl. **batu bane**. Also in KUTA (74), e.g. **nluŋgi muayibi** 'the builder knows', pl. **baluŋgi bayibi**; **musiki ayibi** 'the child knows', pl. **basiki bayibi**.

4. Peculiarities in the shape of nominal prefixes before stems commencing with a

vowel. For example, in FAD (66) the independent prefixes of the u/a gender appear as vį/1 before a vowel, e.g. vįoŋ/loŋ 'antelope(s)', while in BASA (44) the dependent prefix of the bi class appears as ǵu before a vowel, e.g. bisel bi-nan 'our baskets', bisel ǵu-em 'my baskets'.

5. Obscurity in the formation of verbal bases by means of suffixes. For example, in KELE (73) there are four bases in common use, and this is how they appear for the three radicals -buθ- 'break', -laŋ- 'count', and -lum- 'send': -buθa, -buθį, -bume, -buka; -laŋ, -laŋ, -laŋme, -laŋa; -luma, -lumį, -lumįme, lumįka.

6. The frequent occurrence of bases and stems with a final consonant. This is especially characteristic of Groups 40 and 60. For example, in BASA (44) abįpot 'he spoke', abįkek 'he cut'; in BO (42) ŋjoǵ 'elephant'; in YAUNDE (61) ateb 'refusal'. In the other groups the occurrence of final consonants is chiefly limited to nasals, e.g. DUALA (24) įnun 'bird', KUTA (74) ǵįuŋ 'ten'. This feature is much less noticeable in BEDGA (55) and MYENE (71), but even in the former a word like bayamu 'good people' may be heard in some positions as bayam.

7. The occurrence of the combination nl in the speech sounds. An example from KUTA (74) has been given in section 3, and in BO (42) there is nlu 'head', and in FAD (66) nlo 'river'.

Summary

The languages of this zone are different in many ways from those of other zones. In certain respects they appear superficially to have features which have been loosely called 'un-Bantu', but from the illustrations given it will have been seen that they fulfil all the criteria laid down in the second chapter. The distribution of the various differentia just described enables the languages to be assorted into groups, but as may be seen from the classified list, there are far too many gaps in our knowledge for the classification to be more than tentative.

ZONE B

GROUP 10	GROUP 30	GROUP 40
11 NZABI	31 FUMU	41 MFINU
12 Sebo	32 Tege	42 BOMA
13 Tsogo	33 Boma	43 TIENE
14 Cira	34 YAKA	44 SAKATA
15 Punu	35 TIO	45 YANZI
16 LUMBU	36 DEE	46 Dgoli
	37 WUMU	47 Diŋa
GROUP 20		48 MBUNU
21 MBEDE		
22 Mbamba		
23 Tsaya		

Characteristics of the Zone

As in the case of Zone A, here too there is a sufficient measure of linguistic relationship to make it useful to describe the features of the zone in detail.

I. *Common Features*

1. The absence of any genders regularly containing words which indicate smallness or bigness. (Also in Zones A and C.)
2. The absence of an extension -u-, and, in most of the languages, of any true passive verbals. SAKATA (44) is an exception to this last statement, having many related radicals of the type -ful- 'open', -mfumful- 'be opened (by)'. (Also in Zones A and C.)
3. The use of single independent nominal prefixes only. (Also in Zones A and C.)
4. The use of extra independent nominal prefixes. For example in LUMBU (16) ĝomikaba 'to the villages' can govern the agreement of a word with a stem like -otso 'all', as ĝootso 'everywhere towards'. In Group 30 there are three prefixed elements of this kind, e.g. in YAKA (34) kunzo 'to the house', munzo 'in the house', ŋanzo 'at the house', but whereas the first two can govern an agreement the third cannot. (Also in Zone H.)
5. The affixing of extra dependent prefixes immediately to the nominal without any use of -a- as in some zones. For example, in LUMBU (16) tsinzubu tsibaramfi 'the houses of the fishermen', or in DEE (36) leyimu lemokeo 'the song of the woman'. (Also in Zones A and C.)
6. The occurrence of dependent tenses without the suffix *-E. This appears to be without exception in this zone, where dependent tenses use a base similar to one of the principal tenses. In most cases there is a distinct tone-pattern for the dependent tense, e.g. in MFINU (41) bamana (_ _) 'they will finish', bamana (‾‾‾) '(that) they should finish'. (Also in Zones A, C, and H.)
7. The fewness of the tense signs, some languages only using one base. The number of tenses is sometimes increased by the use of different tone-patterns, for example, in MFINU (41) there are only four possible shapes for verbal bases, yet with these ten distinct tenses are made. (Also in Zone C.)
8. The rarity of true negative tenses, most of the languages using attached or self-standing particles. For example, in YAKA (34) the particle pe is the sign of the negative statement, as in ataŋgi mukanda pe 'he did not read the book'; and in MFINU (41) it is we, which does not come at the end of the sentence but immediately after the verbal, as in bakee: we yyüo 'they did not watch the spear'. LUMBU (16), on the other hand, does appear to have some negative tenses, e.g. atsefwa 'he is dead', asafwa ĝo 'he is not dead', though even here the self-standing negative word ĝo usually comes at the end of the sentence as well. (Also in Zones A and C.)
9. The use of an infix as a substitute object. Group 30 is peculiar in that there is no infix for the first person singular, e.g. in TIO (35) bamubere 'they hit him', but babere me 'they hit me'. (Also in Zones B and H.)
10. The absence of an alternance k/g in radicals except in first position preceded by a nasal consonant. For example, in MFINU (41) makaa 'charcoal' is not distinct from magaa, but ŋkana 'craw-craw' is distinct from ŋgana 'crocodile'. (Also in Zones A, C, and H.)
11. A five-vowel system, throughout the whole zone. (Also in Zone H.)
12. A single quantity only in radical vowels. In some of the languages of Group 40, however, there is a peculiar kind of vowel quantity in verbal bases which have no

second consonant. For example, in MFINU (41) **oka** 'to be', and **oka:** 'to refuse to reply' (this latter has to be distinguished from **okaa:** 'to fry'); or in SAKATA (44) **ozo** 'to wash' and **ozo:** 'to learn'. (Also in Zones A and C.)

13. Stress on the radical syllable. (Also in Zones C and H.)

14. An alternance of tone on the radical. MFINU (41) is exceptional in only having one possible tone-pattern for each tense, thus whereas in TIO (35) **ofura** 'to pay' and **ofura** 'to descend' have different tonal behaviour, in MFINU this could not happen. (Also in Zones C and H.)

II. *Peculiar Features*

1. The almost equal proportions of the standard vocabularies related to those from each of the three adjacent zones, A, C, and H.

2. Unusual vowel sequences in extensions and suffixes. For example, in LUMBU (16) **unemisi** 'to wound', **usuguḷu** 'to wash'; in WUMU (37) **obirisi** 'to say', **oswoḡozo** 'to enter'; and in BOMA (42) **osik̲ene** 'to surpass'.

3. The prefix to nomino-verbals, which is **u-** or **o-**. This is distinct from any independent nominal prefix, and governs agreements which are not the same as those for the extra independent prefix **ku-**. For example, in LUMBU (16) **uyaba** 'to know'; in YAKA (34) **usala** 'to work'; and in MFINU (41) **oba onde** 'his beginning'.

4. The occurrence of double dependent prefixes in certain types of nominal, e.g. in YAKA (34) **miti mimibwe** 'good trees', **manzo mamabwe** 'good houses'; or in MFINU (41) **leŋko lilinene** 'a big banana'.

5. The anomalous behaviour of the stem for 'two'. For example, in LUMBU (16) **mioḡo mimioli** 'two arms', but **malu mamueli** 'two legs'; and in WUMU (37) **mili miele** 'two legs', but **mako molo** 'two arms'. This does not always occur in Group 40, e.g. in MFINU (41) **mitana mie** 'two valleys', **manjo mue** 'two houses'.

6. The fusion of extensions and suffixes producing abnormal verbal bases, particularly in the eastern half of the zone. For example, in TIO (35) **obie** 'to ripen', **obio** 'to reject'; in MFINU (41) **osibi** 'to whet', **osüe** 'to squeak', **oseu** 'to sit', **osio** 'to slander'; in SAKATA (44) **otui** 'to lack', **ozie** 'to spread', **otou** 'to try', **okuo** 'to pull'; and in MBUNU (48) **okue** 'to go out'.

7. The existence of some unusual alternances, particularly in alveolar consonants in junction with **-i-**. For example, in LUMBU (16) there is an alternance l/r/d, e.g. **bulili** 'lips', **biriri** 'grass', **badidi** 'small people'; and in SAKATA (44) there is an alternance z/ʒ/j, e.g. **ozila** 'to enter', **oʒiba** 'to know', **ojiḡa** 'to bury'.

Summary

Although this zone has some peculiar characteristics which are hardly to be found elsewhere in Bantu languages, yet on the whole it seems to occupy an intermediate position between the three neighbouring zones, A, C, and H. Nevertheless, not only is it necessary to retain it in order to avoid overloading Zones A and C, but there is a sufficient linguistic distinction shown by the bunching of the isoglosses along its boundaries to make Zone B a very useful set of groups.

THE CLASSIFICATION OF

ZONE C

GROUP 10	GROUP 30	GROUP 60
11 BUŊGILI	31 ŊGOMBE	61 MOŊGO-ŊKUNDU
12 Bukoŋgo	32 Buela	61a MOŊGO
13 Kaka	33 Batį	61b ŊKUNDU
14 Gundį		61c Paŋga
15 Pande		61d Tįtų
16 Nzelį	GROUP 40	61e Buulį
17 Kota	41 *BUA*	61f Bukala
	42 *AŊBA*	61g Yailįma
		62 Laljạ
		63 ŊGANDU
GROUP 20		
21 BAŊGĮ-LOĮ	GROUP 50	
21a LOĮ	51 Mbesa	
21b BUBAŊGĮ	52 SO	
21c Nųnų	53 PUKI	GROUP 70
22 SEŊGELE	54 LUMBU	71 TETELA
23 Tųmba	55 KILI	72 Kųsų
24 Buljạ	56 Foma	73 ŊKŲTŲ
25 NTUMBA, &c.		74 Yela
25a NTUMBA		75 KELA
25b Waŋgata		
25c Mpama		
26 LUSEŊGO		GROUP 80
26a POTO		81 Deŋgese
26b MPESA		82 Soŋgomeno
26c MBŲDZA		83 BUSOŊO
26d *MAŊGALA*		84 Lele
26e BULUKĮ		85 WOŊGO
26f Kaŋgana		
26g LIKU		
27 BŲJA		

Characteristics of the Zone

Although this zone covers a very large area and is composed of eight groups which contain nearly forty languages, yet these languages display remarkably close relationships. On the west and south the limits of the zone are well defined, but the eastern boundary is somewhat arbitrary, although the languages just over this boundary are sufficiently different to justify their being placed in another zone.

I. *Common Features*

1. The existence of genders regularly containing words which indicate smallness. These do not occur in Groups 10 and 20, but in most of the others, e.g. in TETELA (71) there is the į/tu gender, as ̯samba (for įsamba) 'small village', pl. **tusamba**, but not all the words in such genders express this notion, as there are others in them like **keŋge** (for įkeŋge) 'axe', pl. **tukeŋge**. In ŊGOMBE (31) there is a rather exceptional

use of the **mu/ba** gender for this purpose, e.g. **mulįbuki** 'small parcel', pl. **bamabuki**, where the 'embedded syllables' **-lį-** and **-ma-** have no grammatical function, but belong to the stem of the word. (Also in Zones A and D.)

2. The absence of an extension **-u-**, and in many cases of any true passive verbals. WODGO (85) does, however, have such an extension, which requires the suffix **-o** where other radicals have **-a**, e.g. **ubela** 'to cure', **ubeluo** 'to be cured'. BUBADGĮ (21b) has the extension **-įbu-**, e.g. **atumį** 'he has sent', **atumįbuį** 'he has been sent', while BUDGILI (11) has **-įb-**, e.g. **įkamba** 'to bring', **įkambįba** 'to be brought'. There is, however, an extension **-u-** in a number of these languages, but this forms radicals which express the neuter of those with the extension **-ul-** (or **-un-**) and so may be held to correspond to the **-uk-** of other zones. For example, in NTUMBA (25) **-ųmun-** 'waken (tr.)' **-ųmu-** 'wake up'. (Also in Zone A.)

3. The use of single independent nominal prefixes only. There is one exception to this that has been noted in MPESA (26b) where nominals with monosyllabic stems have a double prefix, e.g. **umutu** 'person', pl. **babatu**. (Also in Zones A, D, and L.)

4. The absence of extra independent prefixes. In most of these languages elements which cannot govern an agreement are used where languages in other zones use extra independent prefixes. For example, in BUBADGĮ (21b) the **u-** in **u-lįkulu lįndaku** 'on the house' cannot control any agreements. Similarly in TETELA (71) there is the element **la-** as in **la-ŋgelų** 'to the village', and **lu-** as in **lu-luųdų** 'in the house', neither of which can govern any agreement. (Also in Zone A.)

5. The affixing of extra dependent prefixes immediately to the nominal in Groups 20 and 30. For example, in BUBADGĮ (21b) **bįlamba bįmukunzi** 'the chief's clothes'; in DGOMBE (31) **mįjo mįkųmų** 'the chief's affairs'. In most of the other groups this does not happen, e.g. in *BUA* (41) **ŋbalį lakųmų** 'the chief's house', and in TETELA (71) **lukuki laluųdų** 'the door of the house', **kuki įamvųdų** 'the doors of the houses'. KELA (75) is exceptional in using **-nda-** to link the extra dependent prefix to the nominal, e.g. **įsala indaasaŋgu** 'a garden of maize', **buca bundakųmų** 'the chief's head'. (Cf. the adjacent zones for both types of behaviour.)

6. The occurrence of true negative tenses in most of the groups. On the whole there is little regularity in the formation of negative statements in this zone, but here are one or two examples. BUDGILI (11) uses the self-standing particle **ka** at the end of negative sentences in some cases but not in others, e.g. **babuyiba ka** 'they did not know', but even here there is distinction in form in the tense, cf. **bayibakį** 'they knew'. DGOMBE (31) affixes a negative element to the tense, but this varies from tense to tense, e.g. **bupalaka** 'we liked', **buipalaka** 'we did not like', **bupalį** 'we like', **bupalįtį** 'we do not like'. DKŲTŲ (73) and WODGO (85) both have special negative tenses together with a negative particle at the end of the sentence, e.g. in DKŲTŲ **tumpeya** 'we know', **tupeyį ve** 'we don't know', and in WODGO the same two sentences are **bįtu cųmayiba**, **bįtu cųayiba bo**. (Cf. the adjacent zones for similar types of negative construction.)

7. The absence of an alternance **k/g** in radicals except in first position preceded by a nasal consonant. In all the groups of this zone there are cases similar to this example from BUBADGĮ (21b) where **lįkambu** 'affair' is not distinguished from **lįgambu**, but **ŋkolį** 'hostage' is distinct from **ŋgolį** 'string'. (Also in Zones A and B.)

8. A seven-vowel system throughout the whole zone. (Also in Zones A and D.)
9. A single quantity only in radical vowels. (Also in Zones A, B, and D.)
10. Stress on the radical syllable. (Also in Zone B.)
11. Lexical tone on both radical and suffixes. (Also in Zones B, D, and L.)
12. Absence of any tonal distinction in dependent prefixes. There are one or two exceptions to this similar to that found in ŊGOMBE (31), where the dependent prefix i- which is the singular corresponding to bi̦- often has a tone which is distinct from that of the prefix i- the singular of ji̦-, e.g. bi̦pundu bi̦kųmų (_-_ ---) 'the chief's axes' sing: ipundu ikųmų (_-_ ---); ndaku ji̦kųmų (_-_ ---) 'the chief's houses', sing: ndaku ikųmų (_-_ _--). (Also in Zones B and D.)
13. Regularity of tone-pattern in all syntactical relationships. In general there is no tonal modification either to characterize or to indicate syntactical relationship; once the tone-pattern of a word is established in any context it is found to be the same in all other contexts. (Also in Zones D and L.)

II. *Peculiar Features*

1. An abnormally high proportion of the standard vocabularies related to those of other languages within the zone. In some cases two languages, such as BUŊGILI (11) and BUBAŊGI̦ (21b), have as much as 60 per cent. of the standard vocabulary related, but a more average example may be taken from SO (52) which has about 40 per cent. of its vocabulary relatable to that of other languages within the zone, but only 15 per cent. to languages in other zones; in addition, of this 15 per cent. only a mere 3 per cent. is peculiar to SO within its group.

2. A regular system of extensions in which the vowel of the extension -i̦s- is different from that of -il-, e.g. in BUBAŊGI̦ (21b) -tum- 'send', -tumi̦s- 'cause to send', -tumil- 'send to', -kom- 'be adequate', -komi̦s- 'make adequate', -komel- 'be adequate for'.

3. The use of a prefix, both dependent and independent, as the singular corresponding to the prefix bi̦-, which consists of a vowel only. This appears to have only two exceptions in the whole zone, in SEŊGELE (22) where the prefix is ki- (ke-), and in SO (52) where the prefix is k̲i-, or in some forms of the language hi-, e.g. k̲itųtų/ bi̦tųtų 'wall(s)'. In every other language in the zone the corresponding prefix appears to be i-, e.g. in BUBAŊGI̦ (21b) ibuka ine 'a large pounding mortar', pl. bi̦buka bi̦ne. (This is in direct contrast to what happens in some of the languages of Zone B, where the independent prefix is i-, but the dependent prefix is ki-, e.g. in TIO (B.35) iju kinene 'a large pounding mortar', pl. biju binene.)

4. The occurrence of uncommon prefixes in nomino-verbals. Unlike the languages of Zone B, these have a variety of prefixes, but none appears to have the common ku-. For example, in BUŊGILI (11) i̦bumba 'to hide', in ŊGANDU (63) li̦tuma 'to send', and in KELA (75) i̦kenda 'to go', all of which behave like words in the singular of the i̦/ma or li̦/ma gender. In ŊGOMBE (31) there is bubala 'to speak', and in ŊKŲTŲ (73) ntuka 'to draw water', while WOŊGO (85) and *BUA* (41) have the special prefix u- like the languages of Zone B, e.g. WOŊGO, ulika 'to pass'; *BUA*, upaġa 'to say'.

5. A similarity in the shape of the dependent and the independent prefixes. This is one of the most striking features of this zone, where, for example, the dependent

prefixes of the mu/mį gender are usually mu/mį, as in ŊGOMBE (31) **mukanda mundi mubųŋgį**, 'his book is lost', pl. **mįkanda mįndi mįbųŋgį**.

6. The impossibility of using a nominal as a sentence. Unlike the languages of most other zones, these almost always use some kind of copula in similar cases. Here are a few examples, in BUBAŊGĮ (21b) **mubimbį aŋga ntaŋgį** 'the traveller is a fisherman', pl. **babimbį baŋga bantaŋgį**; in ŊGOMBE (31) **įmu mųdį mukanda** 'this is a book', pl. **įmu mįdį mįkanda**; in ŊGANDU (63) **lįne ŋku lįsala lįnami** 'this is my garden', pl. **bane ŋku basala anami**; in KELA (75) **įse ayadį kųmų** 'his father is chief'. In most cases the copula has a dependent prefix, but ŋku in ŊGANDU is an exception.

7. The use of a suffix -i (distinct from -į) in dependent tenses. Here are some examples of it, from BUŊGILI (11) **bataŋgi** '(that) they should count'; from ŊGOMBE (31) **tusoni** '(that) we should write' (cf. **tusonį** 'we have written'); from ŊGANDU (63) **bukambi** '(that) you should work' (cf. **bukambį** 'you have worked'); from TETELA (71) **katuuki** '(that) we should hear'. There are some exceptions to this in Groups 20 and 80, e.g. in BUBAŊGĮ (21b) **nakįta** '(that) I may fall'; and in WOŊGO (85) **buyiba** '(that) they may know'.

8. The use of the two verbal suffixes -į and -akį. (The common suffix of other zones, -įle, does not seem to occur anywhere in this zone.) There are a few exceptions to this, but the following examples will show approximately the distribution of the suffixes: BUŊGILI (11) -lub- 'say', **alubakį** 'he said'; NTUMBA (25) -yįn- 'hate', **bayįnakį** 'they hated'; ŊGOMBE (31) -bal- 'say', **bubalį** 'we have said', **bubalakį** 'we were saying'; *BŲA* (41) -men- 'see', **bamenį** 'they saw'; SO (52) -lųk- 'paddle', **lilųkį** 'I have paddled', **lilųkakį** 'I paddled'; ŊGANDU (63) -uk- 'hear', **aukakį** 'he heard'; ŊKŲTŲ (73) -kįts- 'descend', **tukįtsakį** 'we descended'; WOŊGO (85) -bul- 'strike', **abulį** 'he struck'. KILI (55) on the other hand uses **-įkį** and **-aka**, but not **-akį**, e.g. -kil- 'do', **tukilįkį** and **tuakilaka** 'we did', **tukilį** 'we have done'.

9. The regular occurrence of the 'inverted' relative construction. Since this is similar in most languages, one example will suffice. In WOŊGO (85) the following are typical relative clauses, **mukanda mumalomba bįnu** 'the book you asked for', **mįkanda mįmalomba bįnu** 'the books you asked for'. In these and all similar cases the verbal agrees with the antecedent only, and the subject immediately follows the verbal.

10. A simple consonant system with an almost complete syllabary. In a number of the languages of this zone many of the words which can be related to those in other languages occur with sounds which are almost identical with those used in the starred forms of common Bantu.

Summary

The principal features of the languages of this zone are a simpler grammatical structure than is found in many others, coupled with a simple phonological and tonal system. This may, in fact, be taken to be one of the important areas of Bantu, displaying as it does fairly homogeneous linguistic characteristics which are different in many ways from those of other zones.

THE CLASSIFICATION OF
ZONE D

GROUP 10	GROUP 30	GROUP 60
11 Mbole	31 *PERỊ*	61 NYARUANDA
12 Leŋgola	32 *BỊRA*	62 RUNDI
13 Mịtụkụ	33 *Huku*	63 FULIRO
14 Genya		64 ṢUBI
		65 HAD̦GAZA
	GROUP 40	66 HA
GROUP 20	41 KONZO	67 Vinza
21 *Balị*	42 NDANDỊ	
22 *Amba*	43 Nyaŋga	
23 Kumu		
24 Soŋgola		
25 LEGA	GROUP 50	
26 Zịmba	51 HUNDE	
27 Baŋgubaŋgu	52 Havu	
28 HOROHORO	53 Nyabuŋgu	
	54 BEMBE	
	55 Buyi	
	56 Kabwari	

Characteristics of the Zone

Unlike the three zones already described, this one is of little linguistic significance. There are reasons for not placing any of these groups in the neighbouring zones, but few, apart from geographical contiguity, for making a zone out of them. Moreover, apart from Group 60, our knowledge of the languages of this zone is so fragmentary that even the grouping is in most cases very tentative. For these reasons a mere outline of the distribution of some of the characteristics is all that can be attempted at present.

1. There is insufficient data for the establishing of standard vocabularies for these languages. From the scanty word-lists which are available some of the words which occur here appear to be related to those in languages to the west rather than to the east, e.g. in BEMBE (54) **mbuka** 'village', **mtuba** 'six', and **-bụnd-** 'fight' all correspond to similar words found in Group C.20. In the Sub-Bantu language *Amba* (22) the vocabulary is almost the only thing which entitles it to be put in the list, but this agrees as to both sounds and tones with many words found in the languages of Zone C.

2. Most of the languages appear to have a gender which regularly contains words indicating smallness, usually **ka/tu**. BEMBE (54), however, seems to have a less usual one **hi/bu**, e.g. **hibuka/bubuka** 'small village(s)' (cf. **mbuka/mabuka** 'village(s)').

3. In some of the more northerly languages of this zone there are some unusual genders. For example, *Balị* (21) in addition to the commoner **-/ba, li/ma, i/bi, ku/ma** has others containing words like these, **ụnzị/kụzị** 'village(s)', **lịbu/mubu** 'river(s)', **kụlụlụ/mulụlụ** 'knee(s)', **bịlị/bebịlị** 'rat(s)', **ŋkulị/buŋkulị** 'wife(s)'.

4. In Groups 10, 20, 30, and 50 independent nominals have single prefixes only.

In Group 40 there are double prefixes in which the first part is o-, e-, or a-, e.g. in NDANDỊ (42) omubiri/emibiri 'body(s)'. In Group 60 there are double prefixes with u-, i-, or a- as the first part, e.g. in HA (66) umugezi/imigezi 'river(s)'.

5. In most cases the prefix of nomino-verbals is ku- (or uku-), but in Group 40 it is eri-, e.g. in KONZO (41) erihịka 'to arrive'. In BEMBE (54) there is prefix u- which governs its own special dependent prefix u-, e.g. utenda ube 'your speaking'.

6. Most of the languages in this zone have three extra independent prefixes, as e.g. in HOROHORO (28) haŋkoŋe 'at the river', kuŋkoŋe 'to the river', muŋkoŋe 'in the river'. In LEGA (25) there is the less usual prefix ga- where others have ha-, e.g. galuμzị 'at the river'. The languages of Group 60 also have a fourth prefix of this kind, i-, which is of limited usage, e.g. in HA (66) ibuami 'in the realm'.

7. The extra dependent prefix is added to the nominal in Groups 40 and 60 without any modification of the double prefix, but there is the element -a- in Group 60, whereas in Group 40 this is not always used. For example, in NDANDỊ (42) ebịsandu bịomuntu 'the man's feet' (cf. omuntu 'man'), ebịsandu bịwe 'his feet', but in HA (66) ibitebe biaumuntu (pr. byoomuntu) 'the man's stools', ibitebe biage 'his stools'. In the Sub-Bantu languages of Group 30, since there is no clear system of classes of nominals, there are naturally no dependent prefixes, e.g. in PERỊ (31) ịsu ndae or ae 'his eye(s)', miima ndae or ae 'his heart'.

8. Nominals are used as sentences in some of these languages. For example, in HOROHORO (28) ŋgojị gonsoga 'the rope is a good one', pl. migojị yemisoga, cf. ŋgojị nsoga 'a good rope', pl. migojị misoga. The languages of Groups 40 and 60, however, prefix ni- to the nominal stripped of the first part of its double prefix, e.g. in KONZO (41) nilunyoŋgo 'it is a big pot'.

9. The dependent tenses mostly have a suffix -e, e.g. in LEGA (25) gulole '(that) you may look'. The Sub-Bantu languages of Group 30 have -i, which is distinct from -ị, e.g. in PERỊ (31) aupi '(that) he may know', aupị 'he knows'.

10. The suffix *-ỊLE appears to occur in most of the groups, apart from the Sub-Bantu languages. For example, in LEGA (25) aatendịle 'he said'; and in SUBI (64) tuazimie 'we got lost'.

11. Apart from Group 40, most of these languages have a fairly simple tense system, and this is one of the most important features which distinguishes those in Group 60 from Zone E. For example, HA (66) only has three main tenses, by means of which it is possible simply to refer, without time words, to two different times in the past and one in the future, as tulaabonie 'we saw', tulaabona 'we have just seen', tulabona 'we shall see'.

12. There are true negative tenses in most languages in this zone outside Group 60, e.g. in KONZO (41) mutuagonyịre 'we slept (yesterday)', neg. muatutegonya. In Group 60, however, a negative element may be prefixed, or infixed, to every affirmative tense, e.g. in SUBI tuatemie 'we cut', nhituatemie 'we did not cut'.

13. The relative clause is usually constructed without any linking word. A typical example may be seen in the following sentence from LEGA (25), bịbịla bịguamonịne bịakolokịle 'the palm-trees you saw fell down'.

14. In contrast to the languages of Zone C, there is usually an alternance g/k in radical consonants in these. For example, in many of the languages -gul- 'buy' is distinct from -kul- 'grow', in BEMBE (54), however, this alternance is missing,

probably owing to the fact that whereas the **-g-** of other languages is represented by **-k-**, **-k-** is represented by zero, and these two radicals appear as **-kul-** 'buy' and **-ul-** 'grow'.

15. There is a seven-vowel system in Groups 10–50 and a five-vowel system in Group 60.

16. There are two quantities of vowel in the radical in Groups 20, 40, and 60, e.g. in HOROHORO (28) **ŋgoko** 'chicken' has a quantity distinct from that of **ŋgooko** 'shore', while in HA (66) the quantity of **-kul-** 'grow' is different from that of **-kuul-** 'take out'.

17. There are two quantities of vowel in extensions in some languages, e.g. in HOROHORO (28) the quantity of the vowel in the extension of **-kusuuk-** 'leak' is distinct from that in **-ģuruk-** 'jump'.

18. There appears to be an alternance **u/o** in nominal suffixes throughout the whole zone, which is in contrast to the whole of Zone C, except Group C.50. For example, in Kumu (22) the suffix of **ndabo** 'house' is distinct from that of **mbaku** 'knife'.

19. In Group 60 there are some peculiar combinations of consonants in the pronunciation of syllables which contain a consonant and two vowels. For example, in NYARUANDA (61) **diumuana** '(isuka "hoe") of the child' is heard as **dģumɲana**, while **ibiatsi** 'grass' is pronounced **ibjatsi**.

20. In Groups 40 and 60 the alternances between voiceless and voiced plosives are masked in junction with a nasal consonant. For example, in NDANDĮ (42) **olukimba** 'cloth', pl. **esjoŋgimba**; or in FULIRO (63) **tukagira** 'we did', **ŋgagira** 'I did'; **tutakagira** 'we did not', **ndakagira** 'I did not'.

21. In Group 60 **-k-** immediately preceding a radical commencing with a voiceless plosive is pronounced **-ģ-**, e.g. in HA (66) **ikintu ikito** 'small thing', pr. **ikintu iģito**.

ZONE E

GROUP 10	GROUP 20	GROUP 30
11 NYORO	21 NYAMBO	31 MASABA
12 TORO	22 HAYA	31a GISU
13 NYAŊKOLE	22a ZIBA	31b KISU
14 CIGA	22b Hamba	31c BUKUSU
15 GANDA, &c.	22c Haŋgiro	32 HAŊGA
15a GANDA	22d Nyakisaka	32a WAŊGA
15b Sese	22e Yoza	32b Tsotso
16 SOGA	22f Endaŋgabo	33 NYORE
17 GWERE	22g Bumbira	34 SAAMIA
18 NYALA	22h Mwani	35 NYULI
	23 DZINDZA	
	24 KEREBE	
	25 JITA	

GROUP 40	GROUP 50	GROUP 70
41 RAGOLI	51 KIKUYU	71 POKOMO
42 GUSII	52 EMBU	72 NIKA
43 KURIA	53 MERU	72a GIRYAMA
44 ZANAKI, &c.	54 SARAKA	72b KAUMA
44a ZANAKI	55 KAMBA	72c CONYI
44b ISENYI	56 DAISO	72d DURUMA
44c Ndali		72e RABAI
44d Siora	GROUP 60	73 DIGO
44e Sweta	61 RWO	74 TAITA
44f Kiroba	62 CAGA	74a DABIDA
44g Ikizu	62a HAI	74b SAGALA
44h Girango	62b WUNJO	
44k Simbiti	62c ROMBO	
45 NATA	63 Ruṣa	
46 Sonjo	64 KAHE	
	65 GWENO	

Characteristics of the Zone

The placing of the limits of this zone has been done on a linguistic basis, but it is difficult to describe exactly the features which are peculiar to the zone, since there are exceptions to almost every one. There are many important languages in these groups, and there is a considerable amount of reliable data available, so the grouping is much less tentative than in some other zones. It is most convenient then to take in turn the differentia which determined the grouping and describe their occurrence.

1. The standard vocabularies contain a large proportion of words which can be related to those found in languages of other zones. In the case of KIKUYU (51), for example, it is about 20 per cent.

2. Apart from Groups 60 and 70, each language makes use of genders which regularly contain words indicating smallness or bigness. For example, DZINDZA (23) has **akahuli/utuhuli** 'small egg(s)', (cf. **ihuli/amahuli** 'egg(s)'), and **idzoka/amadzoka** 'big snake(s)' (cf. **indzoka/indzoka** 'snake(s)'); KISU (31b) has **kabono/bubono** 'small knife(s)' (cf. **kumubono/kimibono** 'knife(s)'), and **kuusaala/kimisaala** 'big tree(s)' (cf. **siisaala/biisaala** 'tree(s)'); NATA (45) has **akabuhi/ibibuhi** 'small stone(s)' (cf. **ribuhi/amabuhi** 'stone(s)'), and **ugusiri/amasiri** 'big rope(s)' (cf. **urusiri/casiri** 'rope(s)').

3. In Groups 10–40 independent nominals regularly have double prefixes, mostly of the type with o-, e-, and a- as the first part. For example, in KEREBE (24) **ekintu** 'thing', pl. **ebintu**. In Group 40 the vowels in certain prefixes are indeterminate, being heard as i or e (and u or o) according to the vowel of the radical, e.g. in GUSII (42), **ikirugu/ibirugu** 'chair(s)', **ekenene/ibinene** 'big one(s)', **umurimu/imirimu**, 'work(s)', **omogeka/emegeka** 'mat(s)'. In the other groups the independent prefixes are always single.

4. The prefix of nomino-verbals is **ku-** (or **uku-**, &c.) in all the groups of this zone except 60, where it is **i-**, which behaves like the singular prefix of the i/ma gender, e.g. RWO (61) **illa** 'to look at', or GWENO (65) **iruma** 'to send'.

5. Extra independent prefixes occur in Groups 10–40, but not in Groups 50–70 which have an extra nominal suffix. Here are examples of the suffix, in KIKUYU (51) **mbembe-ịni** 'among the maize' (cf. **mbembe** 'maize'), in KAHE (64) **numbe-ny** 'at the house' (cf. **numba** 'house'), CONYI (72c) **cisima-ni** 'at the well' (cf. **cisima** 'well').

6. Nominals are used as sentences throughout the zone. In GANDA (15) there is a heavier prefix, e.g. **ǵyemikeka** 'they are mats' (cf. **emikeka** 'mats'); in ZIBA (22a) a shorter prefix, e.g. **mahuli** 'they are eggs' (cf. **amahuli** 'eggs'); in NATA (45) the first part of the prefix is replaced by a nasal consonant, e.g. **mbịtụmbi** 'they are stools' (cf. **ibịtụmbi** 'stools'). In many cases **ni-** is prefixed to the nominal, e.g. in WADGA (32a) as in **niemisaala** (pr. **neemisaala**) 'they are trees' (cf. **emisaala** 'trees'); and in GIRYAMA (72a) **nimacuŋba** 'they are oranges' (cf. **macuŋba** 'oranges'). In others the nominal has the same form as in other sentences, e.g. in BUKUSU (31c) **kuno kumukunda kuaŋge** 'this is my garden' (cf. **kumukunda** 'garden'); or in DIGO (73) **higa majembe** 'these are hoes' (cf. **majembe** 'hoes').

7. A suffix **-e** is characteristic of dependent tenses but by no means confined to them. For example, in KURỊA (43) **turente** '(that) we should bring', **turaarente** 'we are going to bring' (cf. **turaarenta** 'we are bringing'); or in SAAMIA (34) **kutandule** '(that) we should tear', **kunatandule** 'we are going to tear', **kuakatandule** 'we shall tear (tomorrow)'. GỤSỊỊ (42) is exceptional in having an indeterminate vowel as a suffix in its dependent tenses; this is heard as **-e** if the radical has **-e-** or **-o-** but otherwise as **-i** (distinct from **-ị**), e.g. **tuguli** (ˉ-ˉ) '(that) we should buy' (cf. **ntuguli** (---ˉ) 'we shall buy'), and **tutebe** (ˉ-ˉ) '(that) we should say' (cf. **ntutebe** (---ˉ) 'we shall say'). The principal exception to this is in Group 60, where the sign of the dependent tenses is sometimes an infix with the suffix **-a**.

8. The suffix *-**ỊLE** occurs in most of the zone, but is absent in Group 60 and much of 70. RAGOLI (41) is unusual in this zone in having **-ị** but not **-ịle**, e.g. **-tụl-** 'forge', **kutụlị** 'we have forged'. In Group 50 there are the two suffixes **-ịle** and **-iite**, e.g. in EMBU (52) **-bul-** 'hit', **nitubuliite** 'we have hit', **nitubulịle** 'we hit (earlier)'.

9. In much of this zone there is an almost unparalleled wealth of tenses. In Groups 10–50 it is frequently possible to refer, without the use of time words, to four different periods of past time and an equal number of future time, e.g. in NYORE (33) there are the following eight tenses of **-sab-** 'ask': **kuasaba** (_ˉ_) 'we asked (long ago)'; **kuasabire** (__ˉ_) 'we asked (yesterday)'; **kusabire** (___ˉ) 'we asked (this morning)', (cf. **kusabire** (_---) 'we have asked'); **kuakasaba** (ˉ___) 'we have just asked'; **kulaasaba** (____) 'we are just going to ask'; **nakusabe** (__ˉˉ) 'we will ask (later to-day); **kuakasabe** (_ˉ_ˉ) 'we will ask (to-morrow)'; **kulisaba** (__ˉˉ) 'we will ask (after to-morrow)'.

10. Apart from Groups 30, 40, and 60 there are true negative tenses in most languages. For example, in JITA (25) **-ta-** is the negative sign, but the negative of **ecikora** 'we are working' is **citakukora**, whereas there is no form like **cikukora** in use. Here are two examples from languages which have no negative tenses, in KISU (31b) the negative sign is **si . . . ta**, e.g. **kulikula kamaki** 'we shall buy eggs', neg. **sikulikula kamaki ta**; and in WUNJO (62b) **lulewona ŋguku** 'we saw a chicken', neg. **lulewona ŋguku pfo**, shows the sign of the negative to be a self-standing word **pfo**.

11. Few of the languages in this zone make use of a copula -li in the formation of principal tenses. The chief exception to this is in Group 30, where forms like this occur, GISU (31a) **kuli kutema** 'we are cutting', but even here SAAMIA (34) agrees with HADGA (32) and NYULI (35) in not using -li in the corresponding tense, which is **kutemaŋga**. The principal use of -li is in clauses with a dependent time reference, as in the following example from DZINDZA (23): **nitukora** 'we are working', **tuakoraga** 'we used to work',**tuali-ho nitukora** 'we were working (at that time)'.

12. There are one or two unusual consonant alternations in this zone. In Group 30 there is k/k̲ in all positions, e.g. KISU (31b) **katiti** 'small ones' (agreeing with **kamakobi** 'debts'), **k̲atiti** 'small one' (agreeing with **kab̲ano** 'small knife'). In Groups 30 and 40 there is ŋg/ŋ in second radical position, e.g. RAGOLI (41) **-doŋgok-** 'be told in detail', **-doŋok-** 'stroll'; and also the uncommon alternance g/ŋ in first radical position in junction with a nasal consonant, e.g. RAGOLI (41) **eŋgono** 'crown of head', **eŋŋono** 'mark of animal's sleeping-place'. In Group 60 there are some peculiar alternances of flapped and lateral consonants in junction with -i-, e.g. WUNJO (62b) **irika** 'to claim', **iɬika** 'to clothe', **iɹika** 'to send', all of which have identical tonal behaviour.

13. There is a seven-vowel system in Groups 40 and 50. Elsewhere there is a five-vowel system except in Group 10, where languages 11–14 have a seven-vowel system and 15–17 a five-vowel system.

14. There are two quantities of radical vowel in the languages of Groups 10–50, but only one in Groups 60 and 70.

15. The alternation between voiced and voiceless plosives is masked in junction with nasal consonants in Groups 30–50. For example, in WADGA (32a) **olukata/tsiŋgata** 'pipe(s)', **olukoba/tsiŋgoba** 'belt(s)'; or in RAGOLI (41) **ululahi/tsi̧ndahi** 'good one(s)' (agreeing with **ulubaho/tsimbaho** 'board(s)'), **ulutanya/tsi̧ndanya** 'red one(s)' (agreeing with the same words).

16. When the second radical consonant is a nasal compound, there is no distinction between a voiced plosive and its corresponding nasal, in junction with a nasal consonant in first position, in most groups except 60 and 70. For example, in RAGOLI (41) **inneŋgo** 'measure' is not distinct from **indeŋgo**.

17. In Groups 40 and 50 -k- in a preradical syllable is heard as -g- if the following consonant is a voiceless one, e.g. in NATA (45) **ikikulu** 'big one' (agreeing with **iki̧geso** 'knife') is heard as **igikulu**. Similarly in KIKUYU (51) the very name of the language is pronounced **gikuyu**.

18. Apart from the two languages JITA (25) and NATA (45), all the languages of the zone make use of lexical tone, and many of them, including even JITA, use a distinction of tone-pattern to differentiate tenses which are otherwise similar, e.g. in JITA (25) **cialiga** (_ _ _) 'we were (yesterday)', **cialiga** (_ ⁻ ⁻) 'we were (before yesterday)'.

19. In Groups 50–70 the tonal system is often very complicated, and it is frequently difficult to relate the speech-tones to the essential tones of the language.

20. In Group 50 the extra dependent prefixes agreeing with nominals in the singular of the **mu/a** gender, the plural of the **mu/mi** gender, and the singular of the **n/n** gender have a different tonal behaviour from those agreeing with nominals in other classes. For example, in KIKUYU (51) **muri̧go uamugeni̧** (_ _ ⁻ _ ⁻ _ _) 'the stranger's load', **miri̧go iamugeni̧** (_ _ ⁻ ⁻ _ _ _) 'the stranger's loads'.

Summary

Although these seven groups have very little in common, yet they do form a convenient zone for reference. The one which has least in common with the others is Group 60, but it would be still less suitable to put it into either of the adjacent zones.

ZONE F

GROUP 10	GROUP 20	GROUP 30
11 TOŊGWE	21 SUKUMA	31 NILAMBA
12 Bende	22 NWAMWESI	32 RIMI
	22a NYANYEMBE	33 LAŊGI
	22b Takama	34 Mbugwe
	22c Kiya	
	22d Mweri	
	23 SUMBWA	
	24 KIMBU	
	25 BUŊGU	

Characteristics of the Zone

This zone is made up of three fairly closely related groups, and most of its boundaries are sharply defined by the coincidence of several isoglosses. Since, however, there are few features which are really peculiar to the zone it is simplest to describe the distribution of the most important characteristics in turn.

1. There are genders in each language which regularly contain words indicating bigness or smallness. For example, in TOŊGWE (11) **kanyonyi/tunyonyi** 'small bird(s)'; in LAŊGI (33) **kalufjo/tulufjo** 'small knife(s)'; RIMI (32) **ijoka/majoka** 'big snake(s)' (cf. **njoka/njoka** 'snake(s)').

2. Independent nominals have double prefixes in most of these languages only when determined. For example, in SUMBWA (23) **amaguta matimbu** 'the oil is good', but **tuagula maguta** 'we bought some oil'. BUŊGU (25) is an exception, e.g. **unti/imiti** 'tree(s)'.

3. Each language uses three extra independent prefixes, except RIMI (32) which appears to have only one **u-**, e.g. **umoŋgo** 'in the river', **unjia** 'on the path', **unyumba** 'to the house'.

4. Usually **ni-** is prefixed to nominals used as sentences, but this is by no means unexceptional. For example, in TOŊGWE (11) **nimakala** or **makala** 'it is charcoal'; SUKUMA (21) **ulu lugoye** 'this is a rope'; RIMI (32) **iji mburi** 'these are goats'; LAŊGI (33) **ulu niludihi** 'this is a rope'.

5. The singular class which has the dependent prefix **li-** has **i-** as its independent prefix. For example, in TOŊGWE (11) **ibala** 'garden'; KIMBU (24) **igi** 'egg'; LAŊGI (33) **ikufa** 'bone'.

6. A suffix **-ire** or **-ile** occurs in each language of the zone.

7. The element **-ag-** or **-ŋga** which is used in tenses referring to actions in progress also occurs in tenses which do not have this kind of reference. For example, in

TODGWE (11) -bumb- 'fill', tuakabumbaŋga 'we filled'; tuabumbaŋga 'we have just filled'; or in SUKUMA (21) tuahambaga 'we have just planted'.

8. In most of these languages there is a complicated but unbalanced tense system, for example, LADGỊ (33) has four distinctions of past time expressed by its tense system, but only one future.

9. The copula is used as a tense formative in a way different from that noted in Zone E. For example, in KIMBU (24) kuali kuabonjle 'we saw (long ago)'; in LADGỊ (33) kutaha turi majị 'we will draw water'; in SUKUMA (21) tutaali kuzeŋga 'we are still building' (where -ta- is a 'negative' element).

10. There are true negative tenses in most of the languages; SUKUMA (21) characteristically has seven simple affirmative tenses but only two simple negative tenses. Here are two other examples, in LADGỊ (33) tuatụŋgịre 'we have just built', neg. sịtukutụŋga (note the form tukutụŋga does not appear to be used in the affirmative); in RIMỊ (32) nakuṛema 'we shall cut', kuṛjuṛema 'we shall not cut' (note there is no affirmative tense with the sign -u- -a).

11. The consonant alternances of these languages do not present many peculiarities, except in the case of RIMỊ (32), which has the unusual alternance ɾ/ṛ/ʁ in which the first sound is flapped, the second a voiceless one-rap 'r', and the third a voiced uvular fricative. This occurs in all positions.

12. There is a seven-vowel system in every language of this zone.

13. There are two quantities of vowel in the radicals throughout the zone, e.g. in TODGWE (11) -teel- 'throw', -tek- 'cook', LADGỊ (33) -loot- 'dream', -lok- 'pass'.

14. There are unusual types of vowel coalescence in these languages, where neither -a- nor -i- in junction with another vowel is heard in speech. For example, in SUKUMA (21) naaiba 'I forgot' is heard as niiba.

15. Apart from BUDGU (25) the junction of a nasal consonant and a voiceless plosive does not correlate with any masking of the alternances. For example, in TODGWE (11) -kulu 'big', mbusị ŋkulu 'big goat'; in RIMỊ (32) -kụpi 'short', ŋgohe kụpi 'short ropes'; but in BUNGU (25) ŋguku 'chicken', cf. akakuku 'small chicken'.

16. Tone is used lexically in all the languages except LADGỊ (33), but even here it is used grammatically. There are frequent examples of tenses which are only distinguished by a difference of tone-pattern, e.g. in SUKUMA (21) tuabalaga (_ ⁻ _ _) 'we counted (earlier to-day)', tuabalaga (⁻ _ _ _) 'we used to count'; or in LADGỊ (33) tuasakịre (_ _ _ ⁻) 'we sought (to-day)', tuasakịre (_ ⁻ _ _) 'we sought (yesterday)'.

17. Verbal prefixes do not all have the same tonal behaviour. Those agreeing with mu- (sing. of ba-), mi-, and n- (sing.) have a behaviour different from all the others. For example, in KIMBU (24) nyuŋgu ialịmilaga (⁻_ ⁻___\) 'the pot is lost', nyuŋgu jịalịmilaga (⁻_ ____\) or in NỊLAMBA (31) mugunda ualimịlue (___ ⁻___) 'the garden is cultivated', migunda ialimịlue (___ ____) 'the gardens are cultivated'.

Summary

As already noted, the boundaries of this zone are well defined, but it will be seen by comparing its characteristics with those of the adjoining ones that no one set of differentia can operate on all sides. Thus it is sharply distinguished from Zone F by its seven-vowel system, its use of two-vowel quantities, and its use of lexical tone in radicals, as well as by certain grammatical features. From Zone E, however, it has to be distinguished by such features as the use of single nominal prefixes, and several characteristics of the tense system.

ZONE G

GROUP 10	GROUP 40	GROUP 60
11 GOGO	41 Tikulu, &c.	61 SAŊGO
12 KAGULU	41a Tikulu	62 HEHE
	41b Mbalazi	63 BENA
	42 SWAHILI	64 PAŊGWA
GROUP 20	42a AMU	65 KIŊGA
21 TUBETA	42b MVITA	66 Wanji
22 AṢU	42c MRIMA	67 Kisi
23 ṢAMBAA	42d UNGUJA	
24 BONDEI	43 PEMBA, &c.	
	43a PHEMBA	
	43b TUMBATU	
GROUP 30	43c HADIMU	
31 ZIGULA	44 KOMORO	
32 DHWELE	44a ŊGAZIJA	
33 ZARAMO	44b Njuani	
34 ŊGULU		
35 RUGURU		
36 Kami	GROUP 50	
37 KUTU	51 POGOLO	
38 VIDUNDA	52 Ndamba	
39 SAGALA		

Characteristics of the Zone

Some of the groups in this zone are more closely related to each other than are others; in particular Group 60 is one on its own, but this is the most convenient zone into which to put it. Since there are few if any features peculiar to this zone, it is simplest to describe the differentia one by one.

1. Although there is insufficient data for the compiling of many standard vocabularies, it seems very likely that there is a rather high proportion of vocabulary common to some of the groups.

2. Genders regularly containing words which express bigness or smallness occur in almost every language, but the form of the prefixes varies greatly. For example, in TUBETA (21) **kasuke/tusuke** 'small cloth(s)' (cf. **suke/suke** 'cloth(s)'); in AṢU (22) **kabuji/bubuji** 'small goats' (cf. **mbuji/mbuji** 'goat(s)'); in ZIGULA (31) **kagola/wagola** 'small knife(s)' (cf. **ŋgola/ŋgola** 'knife(s)'); in RUGURU (35) **ilatsoka/ipfitsoka** 'small snake(s)' (cf. **intsoka/intsoka** 'snake(s)'); and in HEHE (62) **akafugu/utufugu** 'small pot(s)' (cf. **ikifugu/ififugu** 'pot(s)').

3. In Groups 10, 30, and 60 independent nominals have double prefixes, although

in Group 30 this is not the invariable rule. For example, in KAGULU (12) **imusehe/ awasehe** 'old person(s)'; in KUTU (37) **uluzabi/zinzabi** (or **luzabi/inzabi**) 'rope(s)'; in SAŊGO (61) **iḷipịsị/amapịsị** 'egg(s)'.

4. There are extra independent prefixes, except in parts of Groups 20 and 30. For example, in TUBETA (21) **nyumbeni** 'at the house' (cf. **nyumba** 'house'); in SAMBAA (23) **nyumbai** 'at the house' (cf. **nyumba** 'house'); and in ŊGAZIJA (44a) where there is a prefixed element **o-** as well as a suffix, as in **osindoni** 'at the market' (cf. **sindo/zindo** 'market(s)') and in **onyuŋguni** 'in the pot', (cf. **nyuŋgu** 'pot').

5. The nomino-verbal prefix is ordinarily **ku-** (or **uku-**), but in ŊGAZIJA (44a) it is **u-**, e.g. **uhula** 'to buy'; and in SAŊGO (61) it is **ki-** (distinct from the singular prefix of the **ịsị/ịfị** gender), e.g. **kiseŋga** 'to build'.

6. The first person plural prefix which is very useful in some groups as a distinguishing feature is useless here since it varies so greatly. For example, in SAMBAA (23), BONDEI (24), and SAŊGO (61) it is **ti-**, in ŊGAZIJA (44a) it is **ri-**, but in Group 10 and in ŊHWELE (32) and ŊGULU (34) it is **ki-** or **ci-**, whereas in most other cases it is **tu-**.

7. Nominals are used as sentences in most languages of this zone, usually with some modification of the prefix. For example, in KAGULU (12) a single prefix is used, as in **ino suke inoga** 'this is a good cloth' (cf. **isuke** 'cloth'), as also in KỊŊGA (65), e.g. **aka masụta** 'this is oil' (cf. **amasụta** 'oil'). In ŊGAZIJA (44a) there is a prefixed element, e.g. **ŋgomro mhu** 'it is a big river' (cf. **mro** 'river'); while sometimes the prefix is unchanged, e.g. in KUTU (37) **ğano ğamafiŋğa ğaŋğu** 'these are my eggs' (cf. **ğamafiŋğa** 'eggs'), or in PHEMBA (43a) **nti ule lle** 'this tree is a long one', (cf. **nti lle** 'a long tree'). The regular use of the prefixed element **ni-** is apparently confined to Group 20 and SWAHILI (42).

8. The suffix ***-ILE** occurs in most languages except those in Groups 20–40. A peculiar feature of some of these, however, is that although this suffix does not occur in affirmative tenses, it does in negative tenses, e.g. in VIDUNDA (38) **hatukolile** 'we did not work', where the base **-kolile** is not used in any affirmative tense. HEHE (62) is unique in this zone in using **-ile** and **-ite** almost interchangeably, e.g. **-loŋg-** 'speak', **tualoŋgite** or **tualonzile** 'we spoke'.

9. A suffix **-e** is used in dependent tenses in all the languages, but its use in principal tenses is very rare.

10. In parts of Group 40 an indeterminate vowel occurs as a suffix, e.g. in TUMBATU (43b) **-tambuy-** 'understand', **nitambuyu** 'I have understood', **-toŋgoy-** 'speak', **nitoŋgoyo** 'I have spoken', or in ŊGAZIJA (44a) **-som-** 'read', **risomo** 'we have read', **-fuŋg-** 'shut', **rifuŋgu** 'we have shut'.

11. There are negative tenses in most groups, e.g. KAGULU (12) **ciapoŋhola** 'we pierced', neg. **cisapoŋhole**; TUBETA (21) **tuhira** 'we shall work', neg. **setukahire**; ŊGAZIJA (44a) **ŋgariwahao** 'we are building', neg. **kariciwaha**; KỊŊGA (65) **yụtujkona** 'we are going to lie down', neg. **sịtukakone**. The principal exception is GOGO (11) which regularly prefixes **si-** to affirmative tenses as the sign of the negative.

12. In many languages of this zone there is no formal sign for relative clauses, word order alone indicating the nature of the syntactical relationship, e.g. in ŊGAZIJA (44a) **hawono esio nahula** 'he has seen the book I bought' (cf. **nahula esio** 'I bought a book'). ASU (22) uses a difference in tone-pattern to characterize relative

clauses, e.g. **mugeni eneza** (___ _-_) 'the stranger who will come' (cf. **mugeni eneza** (___ -__) 'the stranger will come'). KAGULU (12) is unusual in having tenses in relative clauses which do not occur in main clauses, e.g. **gano mabiki gonihandile** 'these are the trees I planted' (**go-** is a special relative prefix, and the base **-handile** is apparently not used in principal tenses). The relative construction used in SWAHILI (42) is not characteristic of this zone but of Group E.70.

13. Most of the languages of this zone have simple consonant alternances.

14. There is a five-vowel system throughout the zone, except in SAŊGO (61) and ḲIŊGA (65), which have a seven-vowel system.

15. Apart from Group 60, which has two quantities of vowel in radicals, a single quantity is characteristic of the zone.

16. There is a tendency to some form of penultimate prominence in certain languages of Groups 20 and 30. This feature, which is somewhat rare in Bantu languages, is, however, regularly present in the form of stress only in SWAHILI (42); even in the PEMBA Dialect Cluster (43) it is by no means the general rule, e.g. in TUMBATU (43b) **he'neneza** 'he has not replied', **ako'za** 'he will sell'.

17. In Groups 30 and 40 the junction of a nasal consonant with a voiceless plosive is sometimes heard in speech without the plosive, but with strong aspiration, e.g. in RUGURU (35) **-kulu** 'big', **iŋguwo iŋhulu** 'a big cloth'; occasionally a voiceless nasal is heard instead of the aspirated nasal. In Group 60 there is frequently neither a plosive nor any aspiration in the pronunciation of such junctions, e.g. in BENA (63) **-tali** 'tall', **indege inali** 'a tall bird'.

18. Lexical tone on the radical occurs only in Groups 20 and 60, while nominal suffixes have a lexical tone only in Groups 10 and 20. There is grammatical tone in each of these three groups; e.g. in GOGO (11), where the fact that any given tense of a certain shape can only have one tone-pattern shows that there is no lexical tone on the radical, there are three tenses distinguished by tone-pattern alone, as **ciawuya** (_-_) 'we returned (long ago)'; **ciawuya** (_--) 'we returned (yesterday)'; **ciawuya** (__-) 'we have just returned'. In Groups 30 and 40 there is neither lexical nor grammatical tone in most cases.

Summary

There is a clear boundary between parts of this zone and the adjacent ones, as, for example, between Group G.10 and Group F.30, or between Group G.40 and Group P.10. In other cases, however, the relationship across the zone boundary is much closer, as between Group G.20 and Group E.70; nevertheless a considerable measure of linguistic homogeneity is achieved by the formation of this zone.

ZONE H
GROUP 10

11 Vili	16 KOŊGO	16e N.E. KOŊGO
12 Kunyi	16a E. KOŊGO	16f KOŊGO
13 Bembe	16b YOMBE	16g S. KOŊGO
14 Ndiŋgi	16c SUNDI	16h ZOMBO
15 Mboka	16d BWENDE	

GROUP 20	GROUP 30	GROUP 40
21 NDOŊGO	31 YAKA	41 Mbala
22 Mbamba	32 Suku	42 HUŊANA
23 Sama	33 Huŋgu	
24 Ŋgola	34 Tembo	
25 Bolo	35 Mbaŋgala, &c.	
26 Soŋgo	35a Mbaŋgala	
	35b Yoŋgo	
	36 Sinji	

Characteristics of the Zone

The difficulties of this zone are great, in view of the peculiar one-sidedness of the available data. On the one hand the KOŊGO (16) dialects are well known, as to both vocabulary and structure, but apart from NDOŊGO (21) we are faced on the other hand with an almost complete lack of information. This means that the grouping is unreliable, and also that any description of the zone must be scrappy. From what we do know about these languages it seems reasonable to put these four groups into one zone, and here are some of the features which may be said to characterize it.

1. There is a high proportion of vocabulary peculiar to these languages.

2. There are many series of related nominals; an example from KOŊGO (16) was given in Chapter II, and here is one from NDOŊGO (21): -sal- 'sieve', **musari/asari** 'sifter(s)', **musalu/misalu** 'sieve(s)', **risarilu/masarilu** 'sifting-place(s)'. (Cf. Zone B.)

3. Extended radicals are of very frequent occurrence, in most cases being much more common than simple radicals. (Cf. Zone K.)

4. In most languages there are genders which regularly contain words indicating smallness or bigness, e.g. in NDOŊGO (21) **kanzo/tunzo** 'small house(s)' (cf. **nzo/nzo** 'house(s)'). As in this example it is usual for the stem of these words to commence with an element similar in shape to that of the prefix of another class. In KOŊGO (16f) there is the peculiar prefix **fi-** which forms a gender with no plural, e.g. **finzo** 'small house'. (Cf. Zone B.)

5. The independent nominals have a single prefix in all these languages except S. KOŊGO (16g) where we find forms like **ediaki/omaaki** 'egg(s)'.

6. There are extra independent prefixes in this zone, e.g. YAKA (31) has **ha-, ku-,** and **mu-**. KOŊGO (16) is an interesting border-line case, since it uses the prefixes **ba-, ku-,** and **mu-**, as in **bantu** 'on the head' (cf. **ntu** 'head'), but it also forms more commonly peculiar compounds which behave like one word, e.g. **bana-ntu** 'on the head', where **bana-** is identical in shape with the self-standing word **bana** 'that place there'.

7. Groups 10, 30, and 40 frequently have nasal consonants in dependent prefixes such as **mi-**, e.g. in YAKA (31) **miinda miama mimi** 'these lamps of mine'. (Cf. Zone K.)

8. The second person plural prefix is **lu-** or **nu-** throughout the zone, e.g. in KOŊGO (16f) **lutaŋga** 'you read'; in NDOŊGO (21) **nuaniana** 'you have stolen'; in YAKA (31) **luzayi** 'you know'. (Cf. Zones B and R.)

9. Nominals used as sentences have invariable particles prefixed to them, e.g. in KOŊGO (16) **ibata diami** 'it is my village' (cf. **bata/mabata** 'village(s)'). In NDOŊGO (21), however, the invariable nominal can stand as a sentence without any

change of shape, e.g. **ina ialu iami** 'those are my chairs' (cf. **ialu** 'chairs'). In HUDANA (42) there is a modification of the prefix of nominals used as sentences, e.g. **musiŋi wu aamukufi** 'this string is a long one', pl. **misiŋi mi miamikufi** (cf. **musiŋi mukufi** 'long string', pl. **misiŋi mikufi**).

10. The suffix *-E does not occur in dependent tenses in Groups 10 and 30, but is found in Group 20. For example, in KODGO (16f) **luavutuka** '(that) you should return', and in YAKA (31) **tuakota** '(that) we should enter'; but in NDODGO (21) **tukune** '(that) we may plant'. (Cf. Zone L.)

11. The suffix *-ỊLE occurs in all parts of this zone, and is heard as **-ile, -ine, -ele,** or **-ene** according to the vowel of the radical. (Cf. Zone B.)

12. In general true negative tenses do not occur in the languages of this zone. In KODGO (16f) the negative sign is **ka . . . ko**, e.g. **katusumbidi ntumbu ko** 'we have not bought a calabash' (cf. **tusumbidi** 'we have bought'); in NDODGO (21) the negative sign is **kii . . . ee**, and this is sometimes associated with a difference in the dependent prefix, e.g. **kii kaasuririee** 'he has not forged' (cf. **uasurire** 'he has forged'); and in YAKA (31) the sign of the negative is the extra suffix **-ko**, e.g. **tuzayi** 'we know', neg. **tuzayi-ko**.

13. The consonant alternances are not unusual, but, as in some other zones, there is an alternance **k/g** only in junction with nasal consonants. For example, in KODGO (16f) **-kamb-** 'speak' does not have to be distinguished from **-gamb-**, but **ŋkaŋka** 'kindness' is distinct from **ŋganga** 'medicine-man'.

14. There is a five-vowel system throughout the zone.

15. An alternance of vowel quantity appears to occur in most of these languages, e.g. in HUDANA (42) **-beet-** 'strike' has a different quantity of vowel from **-tek-** 'sell'. (Cf. Zones B and R.)

16. There is radical stress in these languages.

17. The tonal systems of this zone are fairly complicated, syntactical tone being very common. One characteristic of Groups 10 and 40, at least, is that although there is lexical tone on the radical, there is none on the nominal suffix. This means that for nominals of any given shape there are never more than two possible tone-patterns in a given context.

ZONE K

GROUP 10	GROUP 20	GROUP 40
11 CIOKWE	21 LOZI	41 TOTELA
12 LUIMBI		42 SUBIA
13 LUCAZI		
14 LUENA	GROUP 30	
15 MBUNDA	31 LUYANA	
16 Nyeŋgo	32 MBOWE	
17 Mbwela	33 Mpukusu	
18 Dkaŋgala	34 Maṣi	
	35 Simaa	
	36 Ṣanjo	
	37 Kwaŋgwa	

THE BANTU LANGUAGES

Characteristics of the Zone

In some respects this zone is half-way between G and L, but there is still good reason for making it, in spite of its curious geographical distribution. One of the weak points of the classification is Group 30, where the available data are altogether inadequate. However, apart from this, the remainder is fairly reliable. It proves most convenient here to describe first the features which are common to all the groups, and then those that are peculiar to one or more of the groups.

I. *Features common to all the Groups*

1. Most of the languages of this zone appear to have a gender **ka/tu** which regularly includes words indicating smallness.
2. There does not seem to be an extension **-u-** in these languages, or even true passive verbals.
3. Three extra independent prefixes **ha-** (or **ba-**), **ku-** and **mu-** occur in all these languages.
4. Nominals are used as sentences, but there are various types of prefix occurring in such words. For example, in LUIMBI (12) **aa mazi** 'this is oil' (cf. **mazi** 'oil'); in LOZI (21) **ze kilitipa** 'these are the knives' (cf. **litipa** 'knives'); in LUYANA (31) **ici ciisamu ecile** 'this is a tall tree' (cf. **ecisamu** 'tree'); in SUBIA (42) **aa makonde** 'these are bananas' (cf. **amakonde** 'bananas').
5. A suffix **-e** occurs in affirmative dependent tenses.
6. The range of tense signs is very varied, and there is little that can be said to be common even to one group. For example, in LUYANA (31), which only has one verbal base, there are these four simple tenses, **tunookayupa** 'we heard', **tunakuyupa** 'we heard (to-day)', **tuliakayupa** 'we shall hear (soon)', **tunambakuyupa** 'we shall hear (after to-day)'; but in MBOWE (32) there are these quite different tenses on a similar base: **tunakuyuva** 'we heard', **natukuyuva** 'we heard (yesterday)', **tuayuva** 'we have heard', **kamatuyuva** 'we are hearing', **matukayuva** 'we shall hear'.
7. There are true negative tenses, and in any given language the negative sign is usually constant. For example, in MBUNDA (15) the negative has the prefixed element **ku-**, as in **kututuŋgu** 'we shall not build' (cf. **tutuŋga** 'we shall build'); in TOTELA (41) the negative sign is **ta-**, but the negative tense corresponding to **tuakatenda** 'we worked' is **tatunakutenda**.
8. There is a five-vowel system.
9. The radical has lexical tone.

II. *Features peculiar to some Groups*

1. The independent nominals have single prefixes in Groups 10–20, but double prefixes in Groups 40–50. For example, in MBOWE (32) **esitondo/eyitondo** 'tree(s)'; and in TOTELA (41) **ecikumba/ezikumba** 'skin(s)'.
2. In parts of Group 20 there is a double dependent prefix in nominals, e.g. in MBUNDA (15) **moko iayihi** 'a long knife', pl. **bimoko biabihi**.
3. The suffix ***-ILE** occurs in Groups 10 and 20 only, where it often forms part of the base of simple past tenses, e.g. in MBUNDA (15) **-kok-** 'pull', **tuakokele** 'we pulled', **-san-** 'call', **tuaşanine** 'we called'.
4. In Group 10 there is a suffix consisting of an indeterminate vowel, which is

distinct from -a. For example, in CIOKWE (11) -lim- 'cultivate', **tunalimi** 'we have just cultivated', -tumb- 'plant', **tunatumbu** 'we have just planted' (cf. **mutulima** 'we are cultivating', **mututumba** 'we are planting'); in LUCAZI (13) -neh- 'bring', **tuanehe** 'we brought', -hit- 'pass', **tuahiti** 'we passed' (cf. **tuaneha** 'we have just brought', **tuahita** 'we have just passed'); or in MBUNDA (15) -tuŋg- 'sew', **tukatuŋgu** 'we usually sew', -ʒol- 'laugh', **tukaʒolo** 'we usually laugh' (cf. **tucituŋga** 'we are still sewing', **tuciʒola** 'we are still laughing').

5. There is an alternance of two quantities of vowel in radicals in Groups 30 and 40 only. For example, in TOTELA (41) the quantity of the vowel in -**bool**- 'return' is distinct from that in -**bon**- 'see'.

6. Although none of the languages of the zone has any stress, there is a slight lengthening of the penultimate vowel in some languages of Group 10, particularly CIOKWE (11) and MBUNDA (15).

7. There are one or two features to note about the pronunciation of junctions of nasal consonants with voiceless plosives. In Group 10 the nasal is not usually pronounced in this case, but the plosive is aspirated, e.g. in LUCAZI (13) **likombo/khombo** 'broom(s)'. In LUYANA (31) a voiceless plosive in junction with a nasal consonant is voiced, which means that the alternance voiceless/voiced does not occur in plosives in this position, e.g. -**cana** 'small', **umboŋgo unjana** 'a small goat'.

8. In Group 10 there is no lexical tone on nominal suffixes. (Cf. Zone H.)

9. Grammatical tone is used to characterize the different forms, but rarely to distinguish them. Here is an exceptional example from MBOWE (32), **katualima** (_-__) 'we did not cultivate (before yesterday)', **katualima** (__-_) 'we did not cultivate (yesterday)', where the corresponding affirmative tenses are different in shape, **tunakulima** (_-___) 'we cultivated (before yesterday)', **natukulima** (-____) 'we cultivated (yesterday)'.

ZONE L

GROUP 10	GROUP 30	GROUP 40
11 PENDE	31 LUBA-LULUA	41 KAONDE
12 Samba	31a LUBA-KASAI	
13 KWESE	31b LULUA	GROUP 50
	31c Laŋge	51 SALAMPASU
	32 KANYOKA	52 LUNDA
GROUP 20	33 LUBA-KATAŊGA	53 LUWUNDA
21 Kete	34 HEMBA	
22 Binji	35 SAŊGA	
23 SOŊGE		GROUP 60
24 LUNA		61 Mbwera
		62 ŊKOYA

Characteristics of the Zone

There is a striking similarity between the languages in these groups, although it is less marked in the case of those in Groups 50 and 60. In general the grammatical features of these languages are those which are usually considered to be typical of

Bantu languages. Here again it proves to be simplest to describe the characteristics in two sets, taking first those which are common to all the groups.

I. *Features common to all the Groups*

1. There is a single prefix in independent nominals.
2. Extra independent prefixes **pa-** (or **ha-**), **ku-**, and **mu-** are in general use, and regularly govern both nominal and verbal agreements.
3. Nominals are rarely used as sentences, some kind of copula being used in most cases. For example, in LUNA (24) there is the element **-i**, which takes a dependent prefix, as in **bai baefi** (pr. **bee beefi**) 'they are thieves'; or in SALAMPASU (51) **adi aponyi** 'they are thieves'.
4. There is the suffix ***-ILE** throughout the zone, though it appears to be missing in SOŊGE (23).
5. There is no alternance **g̱/-** in these languages, since **-g̱-** only occurs in junction with a nasal consonant, while zero consonant only occurs in junction with vowels. The absence of the alternance is clearly seen in the following pair of words from LUBA-KASAI (31a) **lueeso/ŋgeeso** 'pot(s)', where the prefixes can be shown to be **lu/ꞃ**. (The symbol **ꞃ** stands for an indeterminate nasal consonant.)
6. There is a five-vowel system in all languages.
7. There is no stress or other form of word prominence in any language of this zone.
8. When the second radical consonant is a simple nasal, the alternance **l/n** in some extensions is obscured. For example, **-tumin-** 'send to' is not distinct from **-tumil-** in any of these languages.
9. There is an alternance of tone on radicals right through the zone.
10. There is a difference in the tonal behaviour of the dependent verbal prefixes and those for the 1st and 2nd persons. For example, in KAONDE (41) **uapitile** (ˍˍˍˍ) 'he passed' (where **u-** agrees with **muntu** 'person'), **uapitile** (¯ˍˍˍ) 'you (sing.) passed'.

II. *Features peculiar to some Groups*

1. An extension **-u-** occurs in most of the groups, but it is not found in 60. In Group 10 it occurs in the form **-eu-** (**-iu-**), e.g. in KWESE (13) **-val-** 'give birth', **-valeu-** 'be born', **-tum-** 'send', **-tumiu-** 'be sent'; in Group 20 it occurs as part of **-ibu-** (**-ebu-**), e.g. in SOŊGE (23) **-lel-** 'give birth', **-lelebu-** 'be born', **-tum-** 'send', **-tumibu-** 'be sent'; in Group 60 it appears as a long vowel, e.g. in ŊKOYA (62) **-hem-** 'give birth', **-hemuu-** 'be born'.
2. In Groups 50 and 60 there are double dependent prefixes in some nominals. For example, in LUNDA (52) **mutondu uawuwahi** 'a good tree', pl. **mitondu iayiwahi**; or in ŊKOYA (62) **mutondo wautali** 'a tall tree', pl. **bitondo biabitali**.
3. Extra suffixes to verbals, such as **-ko** and **-mo**, occur regularly in Groups 50 and 60, and here and there in Group 30. For example, in ŊKOYA (62) **uaikala-mo** (pr. **weekalamo**) 'he sat in it'.
4. Dependent tenses are formed with a suffix **-e** (**-i** in Group 50) in all groups except 20, where a suffix **-a** is used. Other tenses rarely make use of a suffix **-e** in this zone.
5. The tense systems of most of these languages are simple. Usually there are not

more than two distinctions of past and two of future time expressed by means of tense signs. For example, in KAONDE (41) we find **tuapotele** 'we bought (before to-day)', **tuapota** 'we have just bought', **tusakupota** 'we shall buy (to-day)', **tukapota** 'we shall buy (after to-day)'. This is by no means without exceptions, as in LUNDA (52), where there are four distinct past tenses referring to simple actions.

6. Negative tenses occur in Groups 10–30, but not in 40–60. For example, in KWESE (13), where the negative sign is **-ko**, the negative sometimes corresponds in form to the affirmative, as in **ŋgajiyile** 'I knew', neg. **ŋgajiyile-ko**, but in other tenses there is a special negative form, e.g. **mbaŋguvutuke** 'I will return', **ŋgusiko ŋguvutuka** 'I will not return'. The principal exception occurs in LUBA-KATAŊGA (33) and SAŊGA (35), where the sign of the negative is **ke** which may be used with any tense. In the other languages of Group 30, although the sign of the negative is **ka-** there are true negative tenses which have no corresponding affirmative. In KAONDE (41) the negative sign is **keci ... ne** which is apparently not even attached to the verbal. In LUNDA (52) the negative sign is **hi- ... -ku**, where the first element is affixed to the verbal and the second to the last word in the clause, e.g. **tukuzata mudimu** 'we will do the work', neg. **hitukuzata mudimu-ku**. In ŊKOYA (62) the special base **-fua-ko** receives the dependent prefix, and is followed by the nomino-verbal in **ku-** to express the future negative, e.g. **tukulaba** 'we shall count', neg. **tufua-ko kulaba**; but in other tenses there is the negative sign **ki- ... -ha**, e.g. **tualaba** 'we counted', neg. **kitualaba-ha**.

7. Relative clauses are often constructed by means of dependent suffixes, except in Groups 20, 30, and 50. For example, in LUNA (24) **aakamona** 'he saw', **biakamona-yi** 'when he saw'; or in LUWUNDA (53) **asadil** 'they do', **yisadila-u** '(things) which they do'.

8. There is an alternance of quantity in radical vowels in all of these languages, except those in Group 60.

9. In Group 50 there is no alternance **i/e** or **u/o** in suffixes. For example, in LUWUNDA (53) **ipepu** 'wind' is not distinct from **ipepo**.

10. In each group except 60 there is an alternance of tone on nominal suffixes.

11. Although there are tone-patterns to characterize the tenses in all these languages, it is rare for the grammatical tones to be the sole distinguishing feature. One example of such a distinction does occur, however, in LUNDA (52), e.g. **uakama** (___) 'he went to sleep (yesterday)', **uakama** (_ ⁻ _) 'he is asleep'.

ZONE M

GROUP 10	GROUP 20	GROUP 30
11 PIMBWE	21 WANDA	31 NYIKYUSA
12 Ruŋgwa	22 MWAŊGA	
13 FIPA	23 NYIHA (Nyika)	
14 RUŊGU	24 MALILA	
15 MAMBWE	25 SAFWA	
	26 Iwa	
	27 Tembo	

GROUP 40	GROUP 50	GROUP 60
41 TAABWA, &c.	51 BIISA	61 LENJE
41a TAABWA	52 LALA	62 SOLI
41b Sila	53 SWAKA	63 ILA
42 BEMBA, &c.	54 LAMBA	64 TODGA, &c.
42a BEMBA	55 Seba	64a TODGA
42b Dgoma		64b Toka
42c Lomotua		64c Leya
42d Nwesi		
42e Lembue		

Characteristics of the Zone

This zone is much less homogeneous than the preceding one, but some of the groups in it may equally be said to display most of the typical Bantu features. For descriptive purposes it is most convenient to take various differentia and indicate the distribution of each of them in turn.

1. Almost all of these languages appear to have a gender such as **aka/utu** (or **ka/tu**) which regularly, though not exclusively, contains words indicating things of small size.
2. An extension **-u-**, which expresses a passive, occurs throughout the zone.
3. Double independent nominal prefixes occur in all groups except 60.
4. The extra independent prefixes **pa-, ku-,** and **mu-** appear to be used throughout the zone, and to control both nominal and verbal agreements.
5. Extra suffixes, such as **-po, -ko, -mo,** are used with verbals throughout the zone, and in Groups 30 and 40 they are used with nominals also. For example, in NYIKYUSA (31) **pabutali** 'at a distance', **pabutali-po** 'at a distance from it'.
6. Nominals are regularly used as sentences. In Group 10 the nominal has the same shape as when used with a verbal, e.g. in RUDGU (14) **icisu** 'a knife', **cii icisu** 'this is a knife'. In Groups 20 and 30 a single prefix is used instead of a double one, e.g. in MALILA (24) **ulukusa** 'a rope', **lukusa** 'it is a rope'; the principal exception to this is MWADGA (22), which replaces the first part of the double prefix with **a-**, e.g. **icitala** 'bed', **acitala** 'it is a bed'. In Groups 40 and 50 there is a single prefix with a long vowel, e.g. in TAABWA (41a) **ubusansi** 'mat', **buusansi** 'it is a mat'. In Group 60, where there are no double prefixes, another element is often prefixed, e.g. in ILA (63) **bantu** 'people', **mbantu** 'they are people'.
7. There is a verbal suffix **-e** throughout the zone, and normally this is the sign of affirmative dependent tenses. Rarely it also occurs in principal tenses, e.g. in SOLI (62) **nitukalime** 'we shall cultivate'.
8. A suffix such as **-ile** occurs in all groups except 60, but its actual nature varies. In Groups 10 and 20 it is **-ile** (or **-ile**), but bases formed with it have fewer alternances in the second radical consonant, e.g. in MWADGA (22) **-let-** 'bring' and **-lek-** 'leave', both have the same **-ile** base, **-lesile**. In Group 30 the suffix is **-ile**, but there is no difference in the alternances of the radical consonants. In Groups 40 and 50 the suffix has an indeterminate vowel, being heard as **-ele** in sequence with **-e-** or **-o-**, but otherwise as **-ile**, e.g. in BIISA (51) **-pet-** 'bend' has **-petele**, and **-pat-** 'hate' has **-patile**.
9. Tense signs tend to be numerous in these languages, though BEMBA (42a)

is probably an extreme case with about thirty by means of which distinct one-word affirmative tenses may be formed. One striking feature is the rarity of any element like -ŋga regularly indicating actions in progress. There is such an element in SOLI (62), e.g. **tulalimi** 'we have cultivated', **tulalimiŋga** 'we are cultivating', but as will be seen from this example its use is peculiar, since it appears to be added not to a simple tense, but to one indicating a completed action.

10. In most of the groups there are special negative tenses, but in 10 there is a negative element, such as **-ta-** or **-si-**, which appears to form negative tenses corresponding to the affirmative. Elsewhere the negative tense is often quite distinct from the affirmative, e.g. in NYIKYUSA (31) **afịkịle** 'he has arrived', neg. **akafika**; or in LENJE (61) **tulaakulima** 'we will cultivate', neg. **teetukaliime**.

11. There is an alternance **g/-** in radical consonants in Groups 10–30 but not in the others, the chief exceptions being that it is missing in MAMBWE (15) and 21–3, and is present in TODGA (64). For example, in SAFWA (25) **-gog-** 'kill' is distinct from **-og-** 'wash', but in a language like BEMBA (42a) there is nothing like this.

12. There is no alternance **f/v** or **s/z** in Groups 30 and 40 (or in most of Group 50 and 61, 62). For example, in NYIKYUSA (31) **-sịmb-** 'write' is not distinct from **-zịmb-**, but in Group 20 these might be different radicals.

13. Other alternances which are absent throughout the zone are **l/d, l/r, s/ʃ**.

14. There is a five-vowel system in radicals in Groups 40–60, and a seven-vowel system in Group 30. In the two remaining groups there is a mixture; thus there are seven-vowel systems in 11–14, but a five-vowel system in 15, and 21–3 have five vowels but 24, 25 have seven.

15. There is an alternance of quantity in radical vowels in Groups 30–50 but none in Groups 20 and 60. In Groups 10 there is a mixture, since PIMBWE (11) has no such alternance but 13–15 have.

16. In Groups 40–60 there is an indeterminate alveolar consonant in some post-radical syllables, but in the other groups there is not. For example, in LENJE (61) **-tey-** 'prepare', **-teyel-** 'prepare for', **-tem-** 'cut', **-temen-** 'cut for', which means that this extension has a consonant which is heard as **-n-** or **-l-** according to whether the second consonant of the radical is a nasal or not.

17. In general these languages have no form of word prominence, but although stress appears not to be used anywhere, WANDA (21) and MWADGA (22) have a slight increase in length in the penultimate syllable, e.g. in WANDA (21) **tuakala** 'we have just bought' is pronounced **twa:ka·la**, and **tuakazile** 'we bought' **twa:kazi·le**.

18. The syllable arising from the junction of two vowels usually contains a long vowel, even in those languages which have no alternance of vowel quantity in radicals. For example, in LENJE (61) **muana** 'child' is pronounced **mwa·na**. Similarly vowels in junction with nasal compounds are always pronounced longer, e.g. in TODGA (64a) **-samb-** 'wash' is heard as **-sa·mb-**.

19. NYIKYUSA (31) makes no use of tone, either lexical or grammatical, but elsewhere there is an alternance of tone in radicals, except in FIPA (13) and RUDGU (14), and on nominal suffixes except in PIMBWE (11). In LAMBA (54) and the whole of Group 60, however, there are only three tone-patterns for dissyllabic nominal stems instead of the four that might have been expected if there were a full double alternance.

20. Grammatical tone is frequently the only way of distinguishing tenses which

have identical shape, although Group 60 appears not to have this feature. For example, in MWAŊGA (22) **tuaiza** (ˉˉˉ) 'we have just come', **tuaiza** (ˉ__) 'we came (before yesterday)', **tuaiza** (ˉ-_) 'we shall come (soon)'; or in FIPA (13) **tualimjle** (ˉˉ__) 'we cultivated (before yesterday)', **tualimjle** (ˉ__ˉ) 'we cultivated (yesterday)'.

21. Dependent verbal prefixes, agreeing with a nominal, have a different tonal behaviour from those of the first and second persons. For example, in MAMBWE (15) **amalola** (_ˉ__) 'they will look' (a- agreeing with **antu** 'people'), **tumalola** (ˉˉ__) 'we will look'; or in LENJE (61) **baatafuna** (ˉ___) 'they will chew', **tuatafuna** (_ˉ__) 'they will chew'.

Summary

Although some isoglosses which are important in separating groups elsewhere cut right through the groups in this zone, yet the boundaries are well defined. In some respects too, as will have been noted, there is much in common between these groups, in spite of an apparent lack of homogeneity. For all that, this zone probably illustrates more clearly than others the basic fact that the sorting of groups into zones is primarily geographical, though with as much linguistic justification as possible.

ZONE N

GROUP 10	GROUP 20	GROUP 30
11 MANDA	21 TUMBUKA, &c.	31 NYANJA, &c.
12 ŊGONĮ	21a TUMBUKA	31a NYANJA
13 MATEŊGO	21b POKA	31b CEWA
14 MPOTO	21c KAMAŊGA	31c MAŊANJA
15 TOŊGA	21d Seŋga	32 Mbo
	21e Yombe	33 Mazaro
	21f Fuŋgwe	
	21g Wenya	GROUP 40
	21h Lambia	41 NSEŊGA
	21k Wandia	42 KUNDA
		43 NYUŊGWE
		44 SENA
		45 Rue
		46 Podzo

Characteristics of the Zone

The groups which constitute this zone have many similarities to one another, and in most cases they are quite different from the neighbouring ones in other zones. In spite of this it proves to be of little value to attempt to distinguish the features which are common to every group from those which are not. Instead the distribution of certain differentia will be described in turn.

1. In Group 10 the independent prefix which serves as the singular of **mi-** is an indeterminate nasal consonant. For example, in MPOTO (14) **ŋkoŋgo/mikoŋgo**

'tree(s)'. In the other groups this prefix is usually **m-**, e.g. in TUMBUKA (21a) **mlomo/milomo** 'lip(s)'.

2. The independent prefix governing the agreement **li-** is itself **lį-** in Group 10, e.g. in MPOTO (14) **lįhiba ili** 'this broom'. In the other groups it is usually zero, but not infrequently gives rise to modifications in the pronunciation of the first radical consonant. For example, in NYUŊGWE (43) **phiri/mapiri** 'hill(s)', **tsomba/masomba** 'fish(es)'.

3. An extension **-u-** occurs in each group, but it is used by itself in Groups 10 and 20 only, e.g. in TUMBUKA (21a) **-kom-** 'kill', **-komu-** 'be killed'. In Group 30 it occurs in the longer form **-iu-** (or **-eu-**), e.g. in NYUŊGWE (43) **-ġur-** 'buy', **-ġuriu-** 'be bought'. In Group 30 it is part of the compound extension **-idu-** (or **-edu-**), e.g. in NYANJA (31a) **-maŋg-** 'tie', **-maŋgidu-** 'be tied'.

4. Independent nominals have single prefixes throughout the zone.

5. There are extra independent prefixes capable of governing both nominal and verbal agreements, such as **pa-**, **ku-**, and **mu-**, in each language.

6. Double dependent prefixes occur here and there, but without any regularity. For example, in NYANJA (31a) certain stems behave like **-tari** in these examples, but others do not, **cintu cacitari** 'a long thing', pl. **zintu zazitari**.

7. The first person plural verbal prefix is **ti-** right through the zone. The only exception occurs in MATEŊGO (13), where the prefix **tu-** is used with future tenses, but even here **ti-** is used with past tenses, e.g. **tuseŋġa** 'we shall build', **tiseŋġite** 'we have built'.

8. Nominals are used as sentences, but usually have **ni-** or **ndi-** prefixed to them in this case. In Group 10 the use of **ni-** is by no means without exception, e.g. in MPOTO (14) **luġoye** 'a rope', **niluġoye** or **luġoye** 'it is a rope'. In TUMBUKA (21) a nasal consonant is prefixed in most cases, e.g. **cijaro** 'a door', **ncijaro** 'it is a door'.

9. A suffix **-e** is the usual sign of the dependent tense, and in some cases it is also used to form the base of principal tenses.

10. There is no suffix like **-ile** in Groups 20-40. In Group 10 there is a mixture of suffixes, but **-ile** only occurs in a few bases in MPOTO (14). In MANDA (11) there is a suffix **-įtį**, e.g. **-tot-** 'sew', **titotįtį** 'we sewed'; in ŊGONĮ (12) there is **-į**, e.g. **-jeŋg-** 'build', **tijeŋġį** 'we built'; while in MATEŊGO (13) there is regularly **-įte**, e.g. **-phal-** 'pull', **tiphalįte** 'we pulled'.

11. In most of these languages there are few distinctions of time expressed by the tense signs, the principal exception being MANDA (11), where there are four distinct past tenses and four future.

12. Actions in progress are mostly referred to by means of the nomino-verbal in **ku-** together with a copula **-li**, e.g. in NYANJA (31a) **-fun-** 'search', **tinafuna** 'we searched', **tinali kufuna** 'we were searching'.

13. True negative tenses are uncommon, elements either being affixed to the verbal or occurring elsewhere in the clause as self-standing words. NYANJA (31a) provides examples of the former type, e.g. **tinapita** 'we passed', neg. **sitinapita**. The second type occurs in MANDA (11) **tiletįtį kibiga** 'we brought a pot', neg. **tiletįtį kibiga lipa**; and in TUMBUKA (21a) **tikawona zovu** 'we saw an elephant', neg. **kuti tikawona zovu cara**.

14. There is usually no special word or element to indicate the relative construction, though in some languages there is a special tone-pattern for tenses in relative clauses.

15. Alternances of the type p/ph occur in first radical position in most of these languages. For example, in TUMBUKA (21a) -par- 'scrape', -phar- 'tell', or in NYANJA (31a) -pit- 'pass', -phik- 'cook'.

16. An alternance l/d is found in this zone, as, for example, in NYANJA (31a), where -lul- 'froth up' is distinct from -dul- 'cut across'.

17. Radicals commencing with nasal compounds are found in verbal bases in some of these languages. This is rare in Bantu languages. For example, in TUMBUKA (21a) -ŋgir- 'enter', or in NYANJA (31a) -mver- 'obey'.

18. TUMBUKA (21a) is peculiar in having the alternances p/b/b̲ and k/g/g̲, e.g. -par- 'scrape', -bab- 'give birth to', -b̲ab̲- 'irritate'.

19. In Group 10 there are seven-vowel systems, but elsewhere only five vowels are found in radicals.

20. There is no alternance of quantity in any of these languages.

21. The languages of this zone are notable for the different voiced labial sounds that occur in them. In MANDA (11) there is a labio-dental semi-vowel, e.g. -ʋik- 'put', where the first consonant appears to be distinct from -w-. In TOŊGA (15) there is a labio-dental plosive which is distinct from the bilabial plosive, e.g. -ɓar- 'shine', -bar- 'give birth to'. In POKA (21b) there is a 'v' without friction, which is distinct from both w and v, as in -ṽur- 'lack'. In NSEŊGA (41) there is a fricative 'w' which has to be distinguished from the pure w, e.g. -w̲ir- 'proclaim', -wir- 'sew'.

22. There is no form of word prominence in Groups 10–20, 40, but in Group 30 there is penultimate vowel length, which is confined to the last word in the sentence. For example, in NYANJA (31a) tadula 'we have cut', pr. tadu·la; tadula ŋkuni 'we have cut firewood', pr. tadula ŋkhu·ni; tadula ŋkuni kumudzi 'we have cut firewood by the village', pr. tadula ŋkhuni kumu·dzi.

23. In the languages of this zone syllables arising from the coalescence of two or more vowels do not usually contain long vowels, e.g. in TUMBUKA (21a) muana 'child' is pronounced mwana. This is not without exception, especially when the two vowels are similar and both are grammatical elements, e.g. in NYANJA (31a) the following two words have the same number of syllables, but the first syllable in the first is distinctly longer than that in the second: aaseka 'they have laughed', aseka 'they laugh'. On the other hand, vowels in junction with nasal compounds are never pronounced with increased length in these languages; thus the first vowel in these two words has the same length in MPOTO (14) njoka 'snake', ŋkoŋgo 'tree'.

24. A nasal compound containing a voiceless consonant is usually aspirated in these languages. For example, in NYANJA (31a) mpasa 'mats' (pl. of lupasa) is pronounced mphasa. In Group 10 this also happens in the singular of the n/mi gender, e.g. in MANDA (11) ŋkoŋgo 'tree' (sing. of mikoŋgo) is pronounced ŋkhoŋgo.

25. In TOŊGA (15) and TUMBUKA (21) there are some special speech sounds which arise from double junctions of the following kinds, as in TUMBUKA (21a) kupua 'to dry up', pr. kupχa; kupia 'to get burnt', pr. kupça.

26. There is an alternance of tone on the radical in MANDA (11) only in this zone. In NYANJA (31a) there is an alternance of tone on nominal suffixes, giving rise to two

tone-patterns in nominals with disyllabic stem. In TUMBUKA (21) tone is not used at all, but in most of the other groups grammatical tone plays a not inconsiderable part in distinguishing tenses, as, for example, in MANDA (11) **tapitįte** (__ ⁻⁻) 'we passed (before yesterday)', **tapitįte** (__ ⁻_) 'we passed (yesterday)'; **yatipitaye** (_____) 'we shall pass (later to-day)', **yatipitaye** (__ ⁻__) 'we shall pass (to-morrow)'.

ZONE P

GROUP 10	GROUP 20	GROUP 30
11 NDEŊGEREKO	21 YAO	31 MAKUA
12 RUĮHĮ	22 MWERA	32 LOMWE
13 MATŲMBI	23 MAKONDE	33 ŊGULU
14 ŊGĮNDO	24 NDONDE	34 Cuabo
15 MBUŊGA	25 MAḆIHA	

Characteristics of the Zone

Although this zone is made up of three groups only, the relationship between them is by no means uniform. Between Groups 10 and 20 it is fairly close, but 30 is in many respects a group on its own. On the other hand, the languages of these groups have more in common with one another than with those in adjacent zones, and it is this fact that justifies the formation of the zone.

1. There are high percentages of related words in the standard vocabularies of Groups 10 and 20, but one notable thing about the lexical characteristics of these languages is the occurrence of common words which appear to have no counterparts elsewhere. For example, the words **kiribi/įribi** 'thing(s)' are found in Group 10, but are not known to be related to words in any language outside the group. The word **ncece** (or **mceece**) for 'four' is characteristic of the whole zone, and is peculiar to it, but at the same time it illustrates the danger of using isolated words for purposes of classification. NDEŊGEREKO (11) and RUĮHĮ (12), which are very closely related to the rest of the group in other ways, happen not to have this word, while POGOLO (G.51), which has little in common with the languages of this zone, does use **mcece** for 'four'.

2. There is an extension **-u-** serving to express the passive in Group 20 only. In Group 30 there is also an extension **-u-**, but since this forms radicals which express the neuter of those with **-ul-** it may be held to correspond to the **-uk-** of other languages. For example, in ŊGULU (33) **-wahul-** 'tear', **-wahu-** 'get torn'.

3. Independent prefixes are single throughout the zone, but in Group 20 some double dependent prefixes occur, e.g. in YAO (21) **litala lialijipi** 'short path', pl. **matala ġaamajipi**.

4. The independent prefix which serves as the singular to **mi-** is either **m-** or an indeterminate nasal consonant in each of these languages. For example, in MAKUA (31) **mhuko/mihuko** 'bag(s); and in MAKONDE (23) **nnandi/milandi** 'tree(s)'. In some of the languages of Group 30 a longer prefix **mu-** is also used, e.g. in ŊGULU (33) **muteko/miteko** 'work(s)'.

5. Throughout the zone extra independent prefixes occur, but in Group 30 they

THE BANTU LANGUAGES 63

are usually accompanied by an extra suffix -ni, e.g. in LOMWE (32) muhice 'river', mmuhice-ni 'in the river'.

6. The nomino-verbal prefix is ku- in Groups 10 and 20, but in 30 it is u- or o-.

7. The verbal prefix for the first person plural is tu- in Groups 10 and 20, but ni- in 30.

8. Nominals are frequently used as sentences in these languages. Sometimes there is an additional element, as in MAKONDE (23), e.g. citale 'iron', ncitale 'it is iron'; sometimes the nominal has the same shape as in other cases, e.g. in MAKUA (31) ila inupa ikina 'this is a small house', inupa ila ikina 'this house is a small one'.

9. A suffix -e is the sign of the dependent tense in all the languages of this zone. It frequently occurs, however, in other tenses too, e.g. in MWERA (22) situtote ŋgubo 'we shall sew the cloth'.

10. There is a suffix -ile in Group 20, although in some cases as MAKONDE (23) it only occurs in negative tenses. In Group 30 there is only the one base, formed with -a, used in principal tenses. In Group 10 -ile does not occur, but -įte is common, though RUĮHĮ (12) uses the very unusual -įke, e.g. -son- 'sew', tusonįke 'we sewed', and in some cases even uses -e as an alternative, e.g. -pit- 'pass', tupitįke or tupite 'we passed'.

11. There are negative tenses in most of these languages. Their form is sometimes related to that of the affirmative, but any relationship varies from tense to tense, and rarely is there a negative corresponding to each affirmative tense. Here is an example from MWERA (22) which may be considered as typical: situceŋge 'we shall build', neg. tukaceŋga; tuaceŋgile 'we built', neg. tukanaaceŋga.

12. Infixed elements serve as substitute objects in each group, but in 30 they are confined to the m/a gender, e.g. in LOMWE (32) yamphwanya 'they found him', but yaphwanya ela 'they found it' (i.e. 'house' empa).

13. Relative clauses are usually identical in shape and tone-pattern with principal clauses, the word order alone indicating whether the clause is relative or not.

14. In Groups 10 and 20 there is no alternance s/z, e.g. in YAO (21) -sito 'heavy' does not have to be distinguished from -zito. In MABIHA (25) and in the whole of Group 30 neither s nor z occurs.

15. In Group 30 only is there an alternance l/r in radicals, e.g. in MAKUA (31) -lik- 'try' is distinct from -rik- 'draw (water)'.

16. An unusual alternance t/tṣ occurs in parts of Group 30, as well as the aspirated th/tṣh, in which the affricates are really predental. For example, in MAKUA (31) itaya 'earth', itṣala 'hunger', ithala 'veranda', itṣhapa 'trap'.

17. In Group 10 there are seven-vowel systems in the radical, but in Groups 20 and 30 only five-vowel systems.

18. There is an alternance of vowel quantity in the radical in Group 20 only, for example, in YAO (21) -jim- 'refuse' is distinct from -jiim- 'stand'. The only exception is DGĮNDO (14) which also has an alternance of quantity, cf. litoosi 'banana' and lugoji 'rope'.

19. The junction of a nasal consonant with the first radical consonant involves the following things in most of Groups 10 and 20. The nasal is not heard before -s-, e.g. in YAO (21) lusasa/sasa 'wall(s)', where sasa is really nsasa. The alternance between a voiceless and a voiced plosive is masked, e.g. in YAO (21) lukosi/ŋgosi

'neck(s)', **lugoji/ŋgoji** 'rope(s)', where **ŋgosi** and **ŋgoji** are really **ŋkosi** and **ŋgoji** respectively.

20. The only form of word prominence occurs in the languages of Group 10 where there is a slight stress on the radical.

21. There are no lexical tones in Groups 10 and 30. In Group 20 there is an alternance of tone on radicals and also on nominal suffixes.

22. Grammatical tone is used to characterize tenses in Groups 10 and 20, but no case has yet been observed where it serves to distinguish them.

23. In Group 20 there is a correlation between tone-patterns and syntactical relationships in some cases, e.g. in YAO (21) **saasu sijaasiice** (⁻⁻ ₋₋⁻₋) 'the firewood is lost', **acila saasu cila sijaasiice** (₋₋₋ ⁻₋ ₋₋ ₋₋⁻₋) 'that firewood is lost'.

ZONE R

GROUP 10	GROUP 20	GROUP 30
11 MBUNDU	21 KUANYAMA	31 HERERO, &c.
12 Ndombe	22 NDOŊGA	31a HERERO
13 Nyaneka		31b Mbandieru
		31c Cimba

GROUP 40
41 YEEI

Characteristics of the Zone

This zone is sharply distinguished from its neighbours, but it is not easy to indicate the features which are peculiar to it. This is largely because the characteristics which separate it from the languages on the north (i.e. in Zone H) are different from those which separate it from those on the east (i.e. Zones K and S). For this reason no attempt is made to divide up the differentia into two sets.

1. In every language there is a gender which regularly, though not exclusively, contains words indicating small things. In MBUNDU (11) it is **oka/otu**, in Groups 20 and 30 it is **oka/ou**, and in YEEI (41) it is **ka/tu**.

2. In most of these languages extended radicals are commoner than simple radicals. Thus in the standard vocabularies of Groups 10 and 20 there are less than 20 per cent. of simple radicals among those used for forming verbals, against the more usual 35 per cent. Examples of these may be seen in the following radicals which do not seem to occur in the unextended form: in MBUNDU (11) **-pitahal-** 'pass', **-talabay-** 'do'.

3. An extension **-u-** appears to occur in all of the languages of the zone, and to express the passive. For example, in KUANYAMA) (21) **-dal-** 'give birth to', **-dalu-** 'be born', or in HERERO (31a) **-hind-** 'send', **-hindu-** 'be sent'.

4. Double independent prefixes occur throughout the zone. In Groups 10–30 the first part of the prefix is usually **o-**, but there are the following exceptions. In every case the class which governs the dependent prefix **li-** has **e-** as its independent prefix, e.g. in NDOŊGA (22) **eyego lioye** 'your tooth'. In MBUNDU (11) the singular of the **omu/oba** and the **omu/obi** genders and the plural of the **omu/oba** and the

e/o̱ba genders only have double prefixes when the stem is monosyllabic or commences with a vowel, e.g. **omuine/o̱biine** 'finger(s)' but **utima/o̱bitima** 'heart(s)'. In Group 20 there are some classes with double prefixes consisting of two identical vowels with no intervening consonant, e.g. in KUANYAMA (21) **onjila/eenjila** 'path(s)', or in NDODGA (22) **osinima/iinima** 'thing(s)'. In YEEI (41) double independent prefixes are apparently used only with monosyllabic stems or with those commencing with a vowel, and even then the same vowel is used in both parts of the prefix, e.g. **umuya/imiya** 'thorn(s)'.

5. Extra independent prefixes, **pa-**, **ku-**, and **mu-** are used in each language. In Groups 10–30 they are added to the double prefix, e.g. in HERERO (31a) **ondundu** 'hill', **kuondundu** (pr. **kondundu**) 'to the hill'. In YEEI (41) in addition to the simple prefix there is also a compound form, e.g. ̱sikali 'chief', **ku̱sikali** 'to the chief', but **muzi** 'village', **kuokumuzi** 'to the village'.

6. In Groups 10–30 extra dependent prefixes also are added to the double prefix, e.g. in MBUNDU (11) **o̱biti** 'trees', **o̱bianja bio̱biti** 'branches of the trees'. In YEEI (41), which does not ordinarily use double prefixes in independent nominals, a similar kind of word occurs through the use of an indeterminate vowel to link the extra dependent prefix. This vowel is heard as **a**, **e**, or **o** according to whether the vowel of the prefix is **-a-** (or zero), **-i-**, or **-u-** respectively, e.g. **murumi/ḇarumi** 'man/men', ̱sipuna ̱siomurumi 'the man's stool', pl. **zipuna ziaḇarumi** (pr. **zaḇarumi**).

7. Double dependent prefixes in certain kinds of nominals regularly occur in Groups 30 and 40. For example, in HERERO (31a) **omuti omusupi** 'a short tree', pl. **omiti omisupi**, or in YEEI (41) ̱sipuna ̱si̱sikuru 'an old stool', pl. **zipuna zizikuru**. Otherwise they only occur in NDODGA (22), e.g. **olutu olunene** 'a big body', pl. **omalutu omanene**.

8. Nominals of one type or another are regularly used as sentences in each group. For example, in MBUNDU (11) **o̱biti** 'trees' or 'they are trees'; or in NDODGA (22) **oŋgulu** 'house', **oŋgulu yianje** 'it is my house'; and in YEEI (41) **dipamba** 'hoe' or 'it is a hoe'.

9. There is a suffix **-e** which serves regularly as the sign of the affirmative dependent tense, but which is rarely used in principal tenses.

10. A suffix **-ile** occurs in each language, but sometimes, as in YEEI (41) apparently, it is more characteristic of relative than of principal clauses.

11. An indeterminate vowel suffix occurs as a tense formative in some of the groups, e.g. in KUANYAMA (21) **ohatuloŋgo** 'we work' (-loŋg- 'work'), **ohatutuŋgu** 'we build' (-tuŋg- 'build').

12. A copula **-li** is rarely used as a tense auxiliary in these languages.

13. The tense signs of the languages in these groups are not numerous, it usually being possible to refer only to one past time and one future time without the use of actual time words.

14. Negative signs are fairly consistent in each language, but the form of the negative tense is often different from that of the affirmative. For example, in MBUNDU (11) **ka-** ... **-ko** is the sign of negative, as in **katuakokele ukolo-ko** 'we did not pull the rope' (cf. **tuakokele ukolo** 'we pulled the rope'), but the negative of **tukoka ukolo** 'we are pulling the rope' is **katukoki ukolo-ko**, and the base **-koki** does not

occur in any affirmative tense. Similarly in HERERO (31a) **ka-** is the negative sign, as in **tumunine** 'we found', neg. **katumunine**, but the negative of **matumuna** 'we find' is **katumuna**.

15. Relative clauses in Group 10 may or may not be introduced by a linking word, e.g. in MBUNDU (11) **esala (elina) tuasaŋga litito** 'the egg we found is small', elsewhere there are extra prefixes agreeing with the antecedent used with relative verbals. The chief exception to this is in NDOꝊGA (22) which uses a special link word formed from the stem **-oka** with **n-** prefixed to the dependent prefix, e.g. **osiloŋga sioka omuhoŋgi esiniŋgi** 'the work the teacher has done', pl. **iiloŋga mbioka aahoŋgi yeyiniŋgi**.

16. There are some unusual alternances in radical consonants in these languages. In Group 20 there is l/d, e.g. in KUANYAMA (21) **-lil-** 'weep', **-dil-** 'be taboo'; as well as the rare d/nd, e.g. **-dudum-** 'growl', **-ndudum-** 'thunder'. In Group 30 there is t/ṭ (and n/ṇ), e.g. **-tak-** 'shake', **-ṭar-** 'look out'.

17. The consonant alternances in radicals are markedly different from those in prefixes in some cases. For example, in MBUNDU (11) b̲ is distinct from both **p** and **m** in radicals, as in **-b̲anj-** 'look at', **-pal-** 'run away', **-mal-** 'finish', but **b̲aonjila** (pr. **b̲onjila**) is not distinct from **paonjila** 'on the path', similarly **ab̲anu** 'people' is not distinct from **amanu**.

18. There is a five-vowel system in the radicals of each language.

19. There is no alternance of quantity in radicals in these languages, but if the vowel of a radical is in junction with a similar vowel in an extension, this may simulate a long vowel. For example, in KUANYAMA (21) where **-fu-ul-** 'strip' appears to have a different quantity from **-ful-** 'rub', but has in fact one syllable more.

20. There is a slight lengthening of the penultimate vowel in MBUNDU (11) but no stress.

21. Tonal data are only available for MBUNDU (11), where there is an alternance of tone on radicals, so that **-kul-** 'plant' and **-kut-** 'tie up' have different tonal behaviour. There is, however, no tonal alternance on nominal suffixes, with the result that nominals have only two possible tone-patterns. Those with disyllabic stem are represented by the typical words **onjila** (⁻__) 'path' and **onjila** (⁻⁻_) 'bird'.

ZONE S

GROUP 10
11 VENḌA

GROUP 20
21 TSWANA
21a ROLOꝊ
21b Kgatla
21c Maŋgwato
22 PIDỊ
23 SUTHU

GROUP 30
31 XHOSA
32 ZULU, &c.
32a ZULU
32b ꝊGONI
33 SWAZI, &c.
34 NDEBELE

Characteristics of the Zone

This zone is different in many ways from most of the others, since it contains only three groups, and these are much better documented than most. The most useful way of dividing up the features would have been to deal first with those common to at least two of the three groups, and then with those peculiar to one group. To do this, however, would have meant duplicating some of the data, so instead the occurrence of each of the features is indicated in turn.

1. In these languages there are a number of radicals consisting of a single consonant only, but no vowel. For example, -n- 'rain' occurs in almost every language. Such radicals are not unknown in other zones, but elsewhere there are rarely more than three of them, whereas the average number in this zone is ten. VENDA (11) is exceptional in having about sixteen, while some of the languages of Group 20 have only six in common use.

2. In Groups 20 and 30 there are no genders which regularly include words indicating small or large things. In VENDA (11) there is a gender ku/zwi in which are found words to refer to small things, e.g. kuḓi/zwiḓi 'small village(s)' (cf. muḓi/miḓi 'village(s)'). A type of word-building which is not common in the other zones described so far gives rise to words of the following type in Groups 20 and 30. In PIDI̧ (22) maruana 'little clouds' (cf. maru 'clouds'), or in XHOSA (31) indluana 'little house' (cf. indlu 'house'), are examples of what are loosely called 'diminutives', but like all other cases where the relationship between words is on the lexical level, it is quite impossible to predict what the so-called diminutive of any given word will be.

3. There is an extension -u- in each group, but in VENDA (11) it usually occurs as part of the compound extension -iu-, e.g. -toḓ- 'seek', -toḓiu- 'be sought'. The peculiar way in which junctions containing -u- are heard in Groups 20 and 30 will be referred to in a later section.

4. Extensions -el- and -is- do not have indeterminate vowels as they do in so many other groups outside this zone. For example, in ZULU (32) -thuŋg- 'sew', -thuŋgel- 'sew for', -ŋgen- 'enter', -ŋgenis- 'cause to enter'.

5. Double independent prefixes occur in Group 20 only, e.g. in ŊGONI (32b) umthi/imithi 'tree(s)'.

6. Extra independent prefixes are not used with any regularity in the languages of this zone. In VENDA (11) they do not occur at all, the extra suffix -ni being used to express a similar meaning, e.g. masimu-ni 'in the gardens' (cf. masimu 'gardens'). In Group 20 there is usually an extra suffix -ŋ, but in some cases an extra prefix is used as well, e.g. in ROLOD (21a) luapi̧ 'sky', muluapi-ŋ 'in the sky'. The agreement governed by such words is peculiar in that it is similar to that governed by the nomino-verbals, as muti-ŋ ḵapi̧tsa 'inside the pot' (cf. pi̧tsa 'pot', ḵutlala ḵapi̧tsa 'the filling up of the pot'). In Group 30 the first part of the double prefix is usually replaced by e- when the extra suffix -ni (or -ini) is used, e.g. in ŊGONI (33b) emgwaɉeni 'in the path' (i.e. emgwaɉa-ini, cf. umgwaɉa 'path').

7. Double dependent prefixes occur in Group 30 only, but the vowel of the first part of the prefix differs from that of the corresponding independent prefix, e.g. in ZULU (32) umuthi omude 'a tall tree', pl. imithi emide.

8. Nominals are used as sentences in most of these languages. In VENḐA (11) ndi- is usually prefixed to the nominal, e.g. micelo 'fruits', ndimicelo 'they are fruits'. In Group 20 independent nominals usually have an element prefixed, but dependent nominals may sometimes have a double prefix, e.g. in ROLOŊ (21a) kimulapo mukulu 'it is a big river', but mulapo mumukulu 'the river is a big one'. In Group 30 there are various ways in which the prefix of nominals is modified when they are used as sentences, but the adding of an extra element is the least common of these.

9. A suffix -e is the sign of the dependent tense in the affirmative in every group, and in Group 10 it also occurs in the negative, e.g. -ful- 'pluck', rifule '(that) we should pluck', neg. risafule.

10. Bases formed with a suffix -ile occur in Groups 20 and 30, but not in VENḐA (11).

11. There are relatively complex tense systems in these languages, but few tense signs. It is rarely possible to indicate a distinction of past or of future time by means of tense signs alone. The number of tenses is increased by the use of the copula to form two-word tenses, as in VENḐA (11) -ṭoḑ- 'seek', roba roṭoḑa 'we were seeking', but also by means of other auxiliaries. Some of the bases used to form the auxiliary verbals are similar to those used in other full words, such as ukuya 'to go' and ukuza 'to come' in ZULU (32). Others, on the other hand, appear only to occur in the form words, as -sali in ROLOŊ (21a), e.g. risali rireka 'we bought some time ago' (-rek- 'buy').

12. The negative sign in verbals occurs regularly in most of these languages, but often there is no affirmative tense which corresponds in form to a given negative. For example, in VENḐA (11) a- is the negative sign, as in riḑibona (‿ ‾ ‾ ‾) 'we usually see' (-bon- 'see'), neg. ariḑibona (‿ ‾ ‾ ‾ ‿); not only are there usually different tone-patterns for the negative tenses, however, but in most cases distinct tense signs too, as in baseha (‾ ‾ ‾) 'they are laughing' (-seh- 'laugh'), neg. abasehi (‿ ‾ ‾ ‾), or in baḑoseha (‾ ‾ ‾ ‾) 'they will laugh', neg. abaŋgaḑoseha (‿ ‾ ‾ ‾ ‿ ‿).

13. Verbals in relative clauses usually have a special form in these languages. For example, in XHOSA (31) there is no link word to introduce a relative clause, but the verbal has a special fixed suffix -yo, and a prefixed element which consists of an indeterminate vowel heard as a, e, or o according as the verbal prefix has a, i, or u respectively, as in into esifuna-yo 'the things we seek', into aβafuna-yo 'the things they seek'. In TSWANA (21) the verbal has the extra suffix -ŋ as well as an extra prefix which agrees with the antecedent, e.g. tshi̧mu iluilima-ŋ 'the garden you are cultivating', pl. di̧tshi̧mu di̧ludi̧lima-ŋ. VENḐA (11) is exceptional in using a link word to introduce relative clauses, which appears to depend in form upon the tense of the verbal, consisting of either -ne or -e with a prefix to agree with the antecedent.

14. In the languages of this zone the consonant alternations in radicals are far more numerous than in any other group. VENḐA (11) probably has the most with at least thirty-seven distinct single consonants in junction with -a- in first radical position, and in addition about eight more in which a nasal is combined with the consonant.

15. Click consonants occur in radicals in Group 30. In SUTHU (23) there is also the alternance c/ch, but in Group 30 there are three series of the type c/ch/gc (in which the third member is voiced). In ŊGONI (33b), an almost extinct member of

the group spoken in northern Nyasaland, this particular series does not occur. Instead there is one in which the clicks have a sort of double sound, being released from a retroflex position and then flapping against the lower teeth.

16. There are seven-vowel systems in Group 20, but five-vowel systems in the other groups. In most cases the number of vowels in speech is two in excess of that in the alternance.

17. There is no alternance of quantity in radical vowels in any of these languages.

18. A striking feature of Groups 10 and 20 is the masking of the alternances of the first radical consonant in junction with certain prefixes. For example, in VENDA (11) alternances such as **t/r** and **k/h** are obscured in junction with the indeterminate nasal consonant, as in **lutaŋga/thaŋga** 'reed(s)' (where the plural is really **ntaŋga** but is heard as **thaŋga**) **luraŋga/thaŋga** 'pumpkin plant(s)' (where the plural is really **nraŋga** but is also heard as **thaŋga**). In junction with zero prefix, which forms words that serve as the singular of others with **ma-**, other alternances such as **r/h** and **dz/l** are masked, as in **ʃaho/maraho** 'buttock(s)', **ʃaɖa/mahaɖa** 'shoulder(s)' (where **ʃaho** and **ʃaɖa** are really ⟩**raho** and ⟩**haɖa** respectively, using the symbol ⟩ for the zero prefix). An example of the masking of the alternance **p/b** in junction with the indeterminate nasal infix is seen in these radicals from SUTHU (23) **-pat-** 'bury', **-mpat-** (i.e. **-npat**) 'bury me', **-bat-** 'strike', **-mpat-** (i.e. **-nbat-**) 'strike me'.

19. In Groups 20 and 30 double junctions in which the middle sound is **-u-** are sometimes heard with quite different consonants. For example, in SUTHU (23) **hulifua** 'to be paid' (cf. **hulifa** 'to pay') is heard as **huliʃwa**; and in XHOSA (31) **ukulumua** 'to be bitten' (cf. **ukuluma** 'to bite') is heard as **ukulunywa**.

20. There is a marked type of word prominence in the languages of this zone, which consists in the lengthening of the penultimate vowel. In Group 20 this is normally confined to the last word in the sentence, but in others it usually occurs in each word.

21. There is an alternance of radical tone in each of these languages, but in Groups 10 and 30 there is a type of alternance which appears to be without parallel in other Bantu languages. Although these are two-tone languages, there are three possible tone-patterns for verbals with simple radicals in certain tenses. Thus in VENDA (11) **-lim-** 'hoe' and **-rum-** 'send' have quite distinct tonal behaviour, and in addition **-baɖ-** 'carve', which is usually similar tonally to **-lim-**, has its own patterns in three or four tenses. In XHOSA (31) also there are three kinds of radical from the point of view of tonal behaviour, thus **-lim-** 'cultivate' and **-thum-** 'send' are tonally quite distinct, but **-ɓoph-** 'bind' which usually behaves like **-thum-** has different patterns in some tenses. This type of threefold tonal alternance distinguishes these groups from all others.[1]

[1] This curious fact may be explained historically by assuming that radicals like the Venḍa -baḍ- and the Xhosa -ɓoph- originally had long vowels, as indeed related radicals do in those languages which have an alternance of vowel quantity. It is found that the tone-patterns of verbals with these radicals are identical with those that are obtained by telescoping similar patterns for radicals with one extension. Thus in Venḍa robaḍa (¯ ¯ _) 'we carved' has a tone-pattern distinct from that of rolima (¯ ¯ ¯) 'we hoed', but if the second and third tones of the patterns of rolimela (¯ ¯ ¯ _) 'we hoed for' are merged, then a similar pattern is obtained. If then -baḍ- originally had a long vowel and behaved tonally like a radical with an extra syllable (as actually happens in many languages of other zones), it is easy to see how the present tonal behaviour arose. An exactly similar explanation will account for the cases where the behaviour of radicals like -ɓoph- in Xhosa differs from those like -thum-. This means that though the alternance of quantity disappeared at some time, the persistence of the extra tone-pattern due to it has caused the emergence of an extra member in the alternance of radical tone in verbals.

70   THE CLASSIFICATION OF

22. There is a difference in the tonal behaviour of the dependent verbal prefixes and those for the first and second persons in each of these languages. For example, in VENDA (11) **bafula** (⁻⁻⁻) 'they forge', **rifula** (_⁻⁻) 'we forge'; in SUTHU (23) **utlabona** (⁻_⁻⁻) 'he will see', **utlabona** (__⁻⁻) 'you (sing.) will see'; or in XHOSA (31) **ɓaɓalile** (⁻___) 'they have counted', **siɓalile** (____) 'we have counted'.

23. In Group 10 the nominal suffix has an alternance of tone but extensions do not; this means that there is a maximum of four patterns for nominals of all lengths. In the other groups there is a tonal alternation both on extensions and on suffixes in nominals, which gives rise to a larger number of possible tone-patterns the longer the stem.

ZONE T

GROUP 10	GROUP 20	GROUP 30
11 KOREKORE, &c.	21 TSWA, &c.	31 COPI
11a Saŋgwe	21a Hleŋgwe	32 TOŊGA
11b KOREKORE	21b TSWA	
11c Tabara	22 GWAMBA	
11d Budya	23 THOŊGA	
12 ZEZURU	23a HLAŊGANU	
13 MANYIKA, &c.	23b Tsoŋga	
13a MANYIKA	23c Joŋga	
13b Tebe	23d Bila	
14 NDAU	24 ROŊGA	
15 KARAŊGA		
16 KALAŊA		

Characteristics of the Zone

In some ways there is a fairly close relationship between Group 20 and the languages of the previous zone. Since, however, the arranging of the groups into zones is largely dictated by convenience of reference, it is preferable to put these three groups into a zone by themselves. The following description of the characteristics follows the same plan as that used in the previous zone.

1. As in the languages of Zone S, there are about ten radicals in most of these languages which consist of a consonant only, as **-n-** 'rain'. In Group 30, however, there are only seven or eight of these radicals, although even this is greatly in excess of the two or three of other zones.

2. There are genders which regularly include words referring to small things in a number of these languages. In 11–13 there is a **ka/tu** gender, and in KARAŊGA (15) **swi/bu**, e.g. **swiŋgurube/buŋgurube** 'small pig(s)' (cf. **ŋgurube/ŋgurube** 'pig(s)'); while in some of the languages of Group 20 there is **ʃi/swi** (or **zwi**), e.g. in TSWA (21) **ʃimutana/zwimitana** 'small village(s)'; comparing these with **muti/miti** 'village(s)', it will be seen that the stem of the first pair is different as well.

3. There is an extension **-u-** in each language. It serves to express the passive, and is used by itself only in Groups 10 and 30, e.g. in ZEZURU (12) **-ras-** 'throw away',

-rasu- 'be thrown away'; or in COPI (31) -woŋg- 'deceive', -woŋgu- 'be deceived'. In Group 20 the extension usually occurs as part of the compound -iu-, e.g. in HLAƊGANU (23a) -kum- 'find', -kumiu- 'be found'.

4. Extensions -el- and -is- occur in Groups 20 and 30 with these vowels, e.g. in ROƊGA (24) -yis- 'carry', -yisel- 'carry for'; -ḇon- 'see', -ḇonis- 'show'. In Group 10, on the other hand, both of the corresponding extensions have the same indeterminate vowel, e.g. in NDAU (14) -par- 'scrape', -parir- 'scrape for', but -pet- 'bend', -peter- 'bend for'; and -kur- 'grow', -kuris- 'cause to grow', but -pon- 'get well', -pones- 'cure'.

5. Independent nominals have single prefixes throughout the zone.

6. Extra independent prefixes occur regularly only in Group 10, where they govern both nominal and verbal agreements. In the other two groups nominals with the extra suffix -ni govern the same agreements as nomino-verbals, which have the prefix ku- or ǥu, e.g. in TOƊGA (32) nyumba-ni ǥuamuntu 'in the house of the man'. COPI (31) in addition to the extra suffix sometimes has the extra prefixes ha- and mu-, but these make no difference to the agreements, e.g. munyumba-ni kuakue 'in his house'.

7. Double dependent prefixes appear to occur in COPI (31) only, e.g. mndoŋga wawunene 'a good tree', pl. mindoŋga yayinene.

8. In Groups 20 and 30 the extra dependent prefix is linked to the nominal with the common -a-, but in Group 10 by an indeterminate vowel. This is heard as a, e, or o according as the vowel of the prefix is a, i (or zero), or u respectively, before the zero prefix which serves as the singular to ba- it is heard as with a, e.g. in ZEZURU (12) musue uetsoko 'the monkey's tail' (tsoko/tsoko 'monkey(s)'), rutsoka ruomunhu 'the person's foot', pl. tsoka dzaḇanhu, but rutsoka ruatenzi 'the master's foot', pl. tsoka dzaḇatenzi. The principal exception to this is in MANYIKA (13) where the linking vowel is usually -e-.

9. Nominals are used as sentences in Group 10 with no modification of the prefix, e.g. in ZEZURU (12) rukoḇa rupami 'a wide river' or 'the river is a wide one'. The principal exception in this group appears to be NDAU (14) which apparently prefers the copula -ri in such cases, e.g. iyi iri mhatso yaŋgu 'this is my house', pl. idzi dziri mhatso dzaŋgu. In the other groups there is usually an additional element prefixed to the nominal, e.g. in ROƊGA (24) bafambi 'travellers', ibafambi 'they are travellers'; in COPI (31) the element is different for independent and dependent nominals, e.g. mndoŋga 'a tree', imndoŋga 'it is a tree', cilo ncacinene 'the thing is a good one', pl. silo nsasinene.

10. A suffix -e is the sign of the dependent tense in the affirmative in Group 10, and in TOƊGA (32) also. In Group 20, however, this suffix is not used, as in COPI (31), e.g. -dzib- 'know', micidziba '(that) you should know', i.e. -ci- -a is the sign of the dependent tense.

11. There is a suffix -ile in Groups 20 and 30, but in COPI (31) -ite is used with those radicals which consist of a consonant only, e.g. -pf- 'hear', hipfite 'we have heard'.

12. The tense systems of these languages are not very complex, and there are relatively few tense signs. At most a double distinction of past time appears possible and a single future time reference, without the use of time words, e.g. in ZEZURU (12) -pind- 'enter', tapinda 'we entered (to-day)', takapinda 'we entered (before to-day)'.

13. The tense signs used in Group 30 are unusual for this zone, e.g. in COPI (31) -hum- 'come out', hidihumile 'we came out', i.e. -di- -ile; hinahuma 'we shall go out', i.e. -na- -a.

14. There are negative tenses in each of the groups of this zone. For example, in TOŊGA (32) the negative sign is **kha-**, as in **hinaba̱la** 'we shall count', neg. **khahinaba̱la,** but there is often a different tense sign as well in the negative, as **hiŋguba̱la** 'we are counting', neg. **khahiba̱li.**

15. Relative clauses are introduced in Group 10 by a special link word consisting of **-a** with the dependent prefix to agree with the antecedent, e.g. in KALADA (16) **cinu ca banu bakayeta** 'the thing the people did', pl. **zwinu zwa banu bakayeta.** In the other groups there is a special fixed suffix to the verbal in many cases, and the clause is introduced by link word. One peculiarity in many of these languages is that some of the tense signs used in relative verbals do not occur in ordinary tenses, e.g. in TOŊGA (32) **nadiwona** 'I saw', **niŋgawona-g̱o** '(which) I saw', where the tense sign **-ŋg̱a- -a** is peculiar to relative verbals.

16. There are very large series of consonant alternations in radicals in these languages, TOŊGA (32) having about thirty distinct single consonants in first radical position.

17. There are five-vowel systems in each of the languages of this zone, but seven different vowel qualities are frequently heard in speech.

18. In Groups 10 and 30 the alternances in the first radical consonant are often masked in junction with certain prefixes. For example, in ZEZURU (12) the alternance **s/ts** is obscured in junction with the zero prefix which has **ma-** as its plural, as in **tsero/masero** 'basket(s)', but **tsara/matsara** 'line(s)', where **tsero** and **tsara** are really ʆ**sero** and ʆ**tsero** respectively. Or in TOŊGA (32) alternations such as **kh/g̱** are masked in junction with the prefix **li-**, e.g. **likhoha/makhoha** 'bat(s)', but **likhokho/mag̱okho** 'coconut(s)' where **likhokho** is really **lig̱okho**.

19. In Groups 10 and 30 the pronunciation of double junctions with **-u-** frequently involves the use of special consonant clusters. For example, in NDAU (14) **muana** 'child' is heard as **mɲana,** while in TOŊGA (32) **g̱ubu̱a** 'to dry up' is heard as **g̱ubg̱wa.**

20. Adequate tonal data is only available for Group 10, where there is tonal alternance on the radical, and on nominal suffixes. Grammatical tone also occurs, and sometimes is the only distinguishing feature in tense formation, e.g. in ZEZURU (12) **ticafamba** (‿ ˉ ‿ ‿) 'we shall travel', **ticafamba** (‿ ˉˉ ‿) 'we are still travelling'.

General Conclusion

Many of the gaps in these descriptions of the characteristics of the different zones are due to the incompleteness of the available data. Others, however, have arisen owing to the limitations imposed by the size of this work. This meant that from the large amount of information collected careful selection had to be made.

In making this selection two main purposes were kept in mind. It was clearly desirable that those who are interested should be able to draw the most important of the isoglosses on their maps. For this reason corresponding features have been described from zone to zone as far as possible.

The main intention of the descriptions and examples, however, was to demonstrate the linguistic basis of the classification. From those which have been given it should have become clear that the group is a unit with a purely linguistic significance, whereas the zone is not. Moreover, they have thrown into relief the element of arbitrariness in the choice of differentia which is inescapable in any grouping of languages. Any who may have looked in vain for some indication of the closeness of the relationship between one group and another should bear in mind that there is no standard against which to measure such relationships. It was, therefore, necessary to avoid expressing any ideas on this subject, since they could not have a truly objective basis.

As has been emphasized from the outset of the work, it is avowedly tentative and experimental. This means chiefly that it lays no claim to finality, but is to be treated as a foundation on which something more permanent may in time be built.

FULL CLASSIFIED LIST OF THE BANTU LANGUAGES

In the following list the first name given for each language is the one which is used by the speakers of that language as far as is known. The others given in parentheses include the most important of those names which have been used at some time or other to refer to it.

Where the prefix to be attached to the form of the name shown here is known, it is placed immediately after it. The fact that in some cases no prefix is given must not be interpreted as meaning that none is used, but simply that up to the present there is no evidence on the point.

ZONE A

GROUP 10
A.11 Ŋgolo
A.12 KUNDU
A.13 Mboŋge (Rombi)
A.14 Lue (W. Kundu)
A.15 LUNDU (Rondo)

GROUP 20
A.21 Mbuku
A.22 KWIRI̧
A.23 SUBU, i̧-
A.24 DU̧ALA (Wuri)

GROUP 30
A.31 BU̧BI, i- (Ediya)

GROUP 40
A.41 Bati (Ceŋga)
A.42 BO (Boŋken)
A.43 Koko
A.44 BASA (Mvela)
A.45 Si̧ki̧
A.46 ŊGUMBA
A.47 Gbea

GROUP 50
A.51 NOHU (Limba)
A.52 Naka (Puku)
A.53 Laŋi̧
A.54 Ŋgumbi (Kombe)
A.55 BEŊGA
A.56 Ṣeke (Bulu)

GROUP 60
A.61 YAU̧NDE (Eundu)
A.62 BU̧LU̧
A.63 Ntum
A.64 Maka
A.65 Zi̧mu (Njiem)
A.66 FAŊ
A.67 Make

GROUP 70
A.71 MYENE, u-
A.71a MPUŊGWE, u- (Mpoŋgwe)
A.71b Ruŋgu, u- (Dyumba)
A.71c GALWA (Ŋkomi)
A.72 DU̧MA, li̧-
A.73 KELE, di̧- (Ŋgomo)
A.74 KUTA, i̧- (Kota, Ṣake)

ZONE B

GROUP 10
B.11 NZABI, bi-
B.12 Ṣebo (W. Kota)
B.13 Tsogo, u-

GROUP 10
B.14 Cira, i- (Ṣaŋgo)
B.15 Punu, yi-
B.16 LUMBU

THE CLASSIFICATION OF THE BANTU LANGUAGES

GROUP 20
- B.21 MBEDE, le- (Mbete, N.E. Teke)
- B.22 Mbamba, le-
- B.23 Tsaya, le-

GROUP 30
- B.31 FUMU, i- (Ŋguŋgulu, E. Teke)
- B.32 Tege, i- (W. Teke)
- B.33 Boma, i-
- B.34 YAKA
- B.35 TIO, i- (S.W. Teke, Lali)
- B.36 ƉEE, esi-
- B.37 WUMU, e- (Wumbu, Mbunu)

GROUP 40
- B.41 MFINU, e- (Funika, Mfunuŋga)
- B.42 BOMA, e- (Buma)
- B.43 TIENE, ke- (Tende)
- B.44 SAKATA, ki- (Lesa, Tete)
- B.45 YANZI, ki-
- B.46 Ŋgoli (Ŋgulu)
- B.47 Diɲa (Dziŋ)
- B.48 MBUNU, gi- (Mbunda)

ZONE C

GROUP 10
- C.11 BUƊGILI
- C.12 Bukoŋgo
- C.13 Kaka (Yaka, Yaŋga)
- C.14 Gundi̧
- C.15 Pande
- C.16 Nzeli̧, li- (Ndzali)
- C.17 Kota

GROUP 20
- C.21 BAƊGI̧-LOI̧
  - C.21a LOI̧
  - C.21b BUBAƊGI̧ (Rebu)
  - C.21c Nu̧nu̧
- C.22 SEƊGELE, ke-
- C.23 Tu̧mba
- C.24 Buli̧a
- C.25 NTUMBA, &c.
  - C.25a NTUMBA, lu-
  - C.25b Waŋgata
  - C.25c Mpama
- C.26 LUSEƊGO
  - C.26a P̱OTO, li̧-
  - C.26b M̱PESA
  - C.26c MBU̱DZA, li̧-
  - C.26d *MAI̧GALA* (Liŋgala)
- C.26e BULUKI̧
- C.26f Kaŋgana
- C.26g LIKU, i-
- C.27 BU̧JA, i-

GROUP 30
- C.31 ƉGOMBE, li̧-
- C.32 Buela (Liŋgi)
- C.33 Bati̧ (Beŋge)

GROUP 40
- C.41 *BUA*, li- (Bali̧, Baŋgo)
- C.42 *AƉBA*, li- (Ŋgelima, Beo, Tuŋgu, Buru)

GROUP 50
- C.51 Mbesa
- C.52 SO, hi- (Soko)
- C.53 PUKI, tu- (Topoke)
- C.54 LUMBU, tu- (Turumbu)
- C.55 KILI, i- (Lokele)
- C.56 Foma, li̧-

GROUP 60

C.61 MOŊGO-ŊKUNDU
  C.61a MOŊGO, lu- (Lolo)
  C.61b ŊKUNDU, lu-
  C.61c Paŋga, i-
  C.61d Tįtu
  C.61e Buulį
  C.61f Bukala
  C.61g Yailįma
C.62 Lalįa
C.63 ŊGANDU

GROUP 70

C.71 TETELA, o- (Suŋgu)
C.72 Kusu (Koŋgola, Fuluka)
C.73 ŊKUTU (Ŋkucu)
C.74 Yela, bo-
C.75 KELA, o- (Lemba)

GROUP 80

C.81 Deŋgese (Ŋkutu)
C.82 Soŋgomeno
C.83 BUŞOŊO (Kuba)
C.84 Lele, usi-
C.85 Woŋgo (Tukoŋgo)

ZONE D

GROUP 10

D.11 Mbole
D.12 Leŋgola
D.13 Mįtuku
D.14 Genya (Enya, Zimba)

GROUP 20

D.21 *Balį* (Bua, Baŋgo)
D.22 *Amba, ku-* (Hamba)
D.23 Kumu
D.24 Soŋgola
D.25 LEGA, ki- (Rega)
D.26 Zįmba
D.27 Baŋgubaŋgu
D.28 HOROHORO, ki- (Guha)

GROUP 30

D.31 PERĮ (Pere)
D.32 BĮRA, *lu-* (Sese, Sumburu)
D.33 *Huku, li-* (Mbuba, Nyari, Bvanuma)

GROUP 40

D.41 KONZO, olu- (Konjo)
D.42 NDANDĮ, oru- (Şu)
D.43 Nyaŋga

GROUP 50

D.51 HUNDE
D.52 Havu
D.53 Nyabuŋgu
D.54 BEMBE, i-
D.55 Buyi
D.56 Kabwari

GROUP 60

D.61 NYARUANDA, uru-
D.62 RUNDI, iki-
D.63 FULIRO
D.64 ŞUBI, uru-
D.65 HAŊGAZA
D.66 HA, iki-
D.67 Vinza

ZONE E

GROUP 10
E.11 NYORO, oru- (Guŋgu, Kyopi)
E.12 TORO, oru-
E.13 NYAṄKOLE, olu- (Hima)
E.14 CIGA, olu-
E.15 GANDA, &c.
  E.15a GANDA, olu-
  E.15b Sese, olu-
E.16 SOGA, olu-
E.17 GWERE, olu-
E.18 NYALA, olu-

GROUP 20
E.21 NYAMBO, eki- (Karagwe)
E.22 HAYA, eki-
  E.22a ZIBA, eki-
  E.22b Hamba
  E.22c Haŋgiro
  E.22d Nyakisaka
  E.22e Yoza
  E.22f Endaŋgabo
  E.22g Bumbira
  E.22h Mwani
E.23 DZINDZA, eci- (Jinja)
E.24 KEREBE, eki-
E.25 JITA, eci- (Kwaya)

GROUP 30
E.31 MASABA
  E.31a GISU, lu-
  E.31b KISU, ulu-
  E.31c BUKUSU, ulu-
E.32 HAṄGA, olu- (Luhya)
  E.32a WAṄGA, olu-
  E.32b Tsotso
E.33 NYORE, olu-
E.34 SAAMIA, olu-
E.35 NYULI, olu-

GROUP 40
E.41 RAGOLI, ulu-
E.42 GỤSỊỊ, iki- (Kisii)
E.43 KURỊA, iki-
E.44 ZANAKỊ, &c.
  E.44a ZANAKỊ, iki-
  E.44b ỊSENYỊ, iki-
  E.44c Ndali
  E.44d Sịora
  E.44e Sweta
  E.44f Kiroba
  E.44g Ịkịzụ
  E.44h Giraŋgo
  E.44k Sịmbịtị
E.45 NATA, iki- (Ikoma)
E.46 Sonjo (Sonyo)

GROUP 50
E.51 KIKUYU (Gikuyu)
E.52 EMBU, ki-
E.53 MERU, ki-
E.54 ṢARAKA
E.55 KAMBA, ki-
E.56 ḌAỊSO, ki-

GROUP 60
E.61 RWO, ki- (Meru)
E.62 CAGA
  E.62a HAI, ki- (Moṣi, Macame)
  E.62b WUNJO, ki- (Maraŋgu)
  E.62c ROMBO, ki-
E.63 Ruṣa
E.64 KAHE, ki-
E.65 GWENO, ki-

E.71 POKOMO, ki- (Pfokomo)
E.72 NIKA
  E.72a GIRYAMA, ki-
  E.72b KAUMA, ki-
  E.72c CONYI, ki-
  E.72d DURUMA, ki-

GROUP 70
  E.72e RABAI, ki-
E.73 DIGO, ki-
E.74 TAITA
  E.74a DABIDA, ki-
  E.74b SAGALA, ki-

ZONE F

GROUP 10
F.11 TODGWE, ki-
F.12 Bende

GROUP 20
F.23 SUMBWA, ki-
F.24 KIMBU, ki-
F.25 BUDGU, iki-

GROUP 20
F.21 SUKUMA, ki-
F.22 NYAMWESI, ki-
  F.22a NYANYEMBE, ki-
  F.22b Takama
  F.22c Kiya
  F.22d Mweri

GROUP 30
F.31 NILAMBA, iki- (Ilamba)
F.32 RIMI, ki- (Nyaturu)
F.33 LADGI, ki- (Irangi)
F.34 Mbugwe

ZONE G

GROUP 10
G.11 GOGO, ci-
G.12 KAGULU, ci- (N. Sagara)

GROUP 30
G.37 KUTU, ki-
G.38 VIDUNDA, ci-
G.39 SAGALA, ki-

GROUP 20
G.21 TUBETA, ki- (Taveta)
G.22 ASU, ci- (Pare)
G.23 SAMBAA, ki- (Sambara)
G.24 BONDEI, ki-

GROUP 40
G.41 Tikulu, &c.
  G.41a Tikulu, ki-
  G.41b Mbalazi, ki-
G.42 SWAHILI, ki-
  G.42a AMU, ki-
  G.42b MVITA, ki-
  G.42c MRIMA, ki-
  G.42d UNGUJA, ki-
G.43 PEMBA, &c.
  G.43a PHEMBA, ki-
  G.43b TUMBATU, ki-
  G.43c HADIMU, ki-
G.44 KOMORO
  G.44a DGAZIJA, ki-
  G.44b Njuani, ki-

GROUP 30
G.31 ZIGULA, ki-
G.32 DHWELE, ki-
G.33 ZARAMO, ki- (Dzalamo)
G.34 DGULU, ki-
G.35 RUGURU, iki-
G.36 Kami, ki-

THE BANTU LANGUAGES

GROUP 50
G.51 POGOLO, ci-
G.52 Ndamba

GROUP 60
G.61 SAŊGO, esi-
G.62 HEHE, eki-
G.63 BENA, eki-
G.64 PAŊGWA, eki-
G.65 KIŊGA, eki-
G.66 Wanji
G.67 Kisi

ZONE H

GROUP 10
H.11 Vili, ki-
H.12 Kunyi
H.13 Bembe
H.14 Ndiŋgi
H.15 Mboka
H.16 KOŊGO
  H.16a E. KOŊGO, ka- (Fiote)
  H.16b YOMBE, ki-
  H.16c SUNDI
  H.16d BWENDE
  H.16e N.E. KOŊGO, ki-
  H.16f KOŊGO, ki-
  H.16g S. KOŊGO, kisi-
  H.16h ZOMBO, ki-

GROUP 20
H.23 Sama, ki-
H.24 Ŋgola
H.25 Bolo, lu- (Haka)
H.26 Soŋgo

GROUP 30
H.31 YAKA, ki-
H.32 Suku, ki-
H.33 Huŋgu
H.34 Tembo
H.35 Mbaŋgala, &c.
  H.35a Mbaŋgala, u-
  H.35b Yoŋgo
H.36 Sinji (Nuŋgo)

GROUP 20
H.21 NDOŊGO, ki- (Mbundu)
H.22 Mbamba

GROUP 40
H.41 Mbala, ki-
H.42 HUŊANA, ki- (Huana)

ZONE K

GROUP 10
K.11 CIOKWE, ci- (Cioko)
K.12 LUIMBI, ci-
K.13 LUCAZI, ci- (Ponda)
K.14 LUENA
K.15 MBUNDA, ci-
K.16 Nyeŋgo
K.17 Mbwela
K.18 Ŋkaŋgala

GROUP 30
K.31 LUYANA, esi- (Luyi)
K.32 MBOWE, esi-
K.33 Mpukusu (Goba)
K.34 Masi
K.35 Simaa
K.36 Sanjo
K.37 Kwaŋgwa

GROUP 20
K.21 LOZI, si- (Kololo)

GROUP 40
K.41 TOTELA, eci-
K.42 SUBIA, eci-

ZONE L

GROUP 10
L.11 PENDE, ki- (Pindi, Pinji)
L.12 Samba, u-
L.13 KWESE, u- (Pindi)

GROUP 20
L.21 Kete, lu-
L.22 Binji
L.23 SODGE, lu- (Yembe)
L.24 LUNA (Iŋkoŋgo)

GROUP 30
L.31 LUBA-LULUA
  L.31a LUBA-KASAI, ci-
  L.31b LULUA
  L.31c Laŋge, cisi-
L.32 KANYOKA
L.33 LUBA-KATADGA, ki-

GROUP 30
L.34 HEMBA, ki-
L.35 SADGA

GROUP 40
L.41 KAONDE, ci- (Kahonde)

GROUP 50
L.51 SALAMPASU
L.52 LUNDA, ci-
L.53 LUWUNDA, ci-

GROUP 60
L.61 Mbwera, ṣi-
L.62 DKOYA, ṣi-

ZONE M

GROUP 10
M.11 PIMBWE, ici-
M.12 Ruŋgwa
M.13 FIPA
M.14 RUDGU
M.15 MAMBWE, ici-

GROUP 20
M.21 WANDA, ici- (Wandia)
M.22 MWADGA, iciina-
M.23 NYIHA, iṣi- (Nyika)
M.24 MALILA, iṣi-
M.25 SAFWA, iṣi-
M.26 Iwa
M.27 Tembo

GROUP 30
M.31 NYIKYỤSA, iki- (Konde, Kukwe, Sokili)

GROUP 40
M.41 TAABWA, &c. (Ruŋgu)
  M.41a TAABWA, ici-
  M.41b Sila
M.42 BEMBA, &c.
  M.42a BEMBA, ici- (Wemba)
  M.42b Dgoma
  M.42c Lomotua
  M.42d Nwesi
  M.42e Lembue

GROUP 50
M.51 BIISA, ici- (Wisa)
M.52 LALA, ici-
M.53 SWAKA, ici-
M.54 LAMBA, ici-
M.55 Seba

GROUP 60
M.61 LENJE, ci- (Ciina Mukuni)
M.62 SOLI, ci-
M.63 ILA, ci- (Sukulumbwe)
M.64 TOŊGA, &c.
  M.64a TOŊGA, ci-
  M.64b Toka
  M.64c Leya

ZONE N

GROUP 10
N.11 MANDA, ci-
N.12 ŊGONI, ci-
N.13 MATEŊGO, ci-
N.14 MPOTO, ci-
N.15 TOŊGA, ci- (Siska)

GROUP 30
N.31 NYANJA, &c.
  N.31a NYANJA, ci-
  N.31b CEWA, ci- (Peta)
  N.31c MAŊANJA, ci-
N.32 Mbo
N.33 Mazaro

GROUP 20
N.21 TUMBUKA, &c.
  N.21a TUMBUKA, ci-
  N.21b POKA, ci-
  N.21c KAMAŊGA, ci- (Heŋga)
  N.21d Seŋga
  N.21e Yombe
  N.21f Fuŋgwe
  N.21g Wenya
  N.21h Lambia
  N.21k Wandia

GROUP 40
N.41 NSEŊGA, ci-
N.42 KUNDA, ci-
N.43 NYUŊGWE, ci- (Tete)
N.44 SENA, ci-
N.45 Rue, ci-
N.46 Podzo, ci-

ZONE P

GROUP 10
P.11 NDEŊGEREKO, ki-
P.12 RUIHI, ki- (Rufiji)
P.13 MATUMBI, ki-
P.14 ŊGINDO, ki-
P.15 MBUŊGA

GROUP 20
P.23 MAKONDE, ci-
P.24 NDONDE, ci-
P.25 MABIHA, ci- (Mavia)

GROUP 20
P.21 YAO, ci-
P.22 MWERA, ci-

GROUP 30
P.31 MAKUA, i-
P.32 LOMWE, i-
P.33 ŊGULU, i-
P.34 Cuabo, ci- (Cuambo)

ZONE R

GROUP 10
R.11 MBUNDU, u- (Nano)
R.12 Ndombe
R.13 Nyaneka

GROUP 20
R.21 KUANYAMA, oci- (Humba)
R.22 NDOŊGA, oci- (Ambo)

GROUP 30
R.31 HERERO, &c.
R.31a HERERO, oci-
R.31b Mbandieru
R.31c Cimba

GROUP 40
R.41 YEEI (Yeye)

ZONE S

GROUP 10
S.11 VENḐA, ci-

GROUP 20
S.21 TSWANA, si- (Cwana)
S.21a ROLOŊ, si-
S.21b Kgatla, si-
S.21c Maŋgwato, si-
S.22 PIDI̦, si- (Pedi)
S.23 SUTHU, si-

GROUP 30
S.31 XHOSA, isi- (Xosa)
S.32 ZULU, &c.
S.32a ZULU, isi-
S.32b ŊGONI, isi-
S.33 SWAZI, &c.
S.34 NDEBELE, isi- (Tebele)

ZONE T

GROUP 10
T.11 KOREKORE, &c.
T.11a Șaŋgwe
T.11b KOREKORE, ci-
T.11c Tabara, ci-
T.11d Budya
T.12 ZEZURU, ci-
T.13 MANYIKA, &c.
T.13a MANYIKA, ci-
T.13b Tebe, ci-
T.14 NDAU, ci- (Sofala)
T.15 KARAŊGA, ci-
T.16 KALAḐA, ci-

GROUP 20
T.21 TSWA, &c.
T.21a Hleŋgwe, și-
T.21b TSWA, și-
T.22 GWAMBA
T.23 THOŊGA
T.23a HLAŊGANU (Șaŋgaan)
T.23b Tsoŋga
T.23c Joŋga
T.23d Bila
T.24 ROŊGA, și-

GROUP 30
T.31 COPI, și- (Leŋge)
T.32 TOŊGA, gi-

INDEX TO THE LANGUAGES

In the following alphabetical index the approximate geographical location of the languages has been indicated by reference to the territory where they are spoken. Here is a list of the abbreviations used:

A.	Angola	P.E.	Portuguese East Africa
B.	Bechuanaland	R.M.	Rio Muni (Spanish Guinea)
C.	Cameroons	R.U.	Ruanda-Urundi
C.B.	Belgian Congo	S.A.	Union of South Africa
C.F.	French Middle Congo	S.R.	Southern Rhodesia
G.	Gaboon	S.W.	South-West Africa
K.	Kenya	T.T.	Tanganyika Territory
N.	Nyasaland	U.	Uganda Protectorate
N.R.	Northern Rhodesia	Z.	Zanzibar Protectorate

Amba (C.B., U.) D.22
Ambo (S.W.) R.22
Amu (K.) G.42a
Aŋba (C.B.) C.42
Aŋgazija (Comoro Is.) G.44a
Aruṣa (T.T.) E.63
Aṣu (T.T.) G.22
Auṣi (N.R.) M.42

Mbala (C.B.) H.41
Mbalazi (Somaliland) G.41b
Ḅale (A., N.R.) K.24
Ḅalị (C.B.) D.21
Mbamba (C.F.) B.22
Mbamba (A.) H.22
Mbandieru (S.W.) R.31b
Mbaŋgala (A.) H.35a
Baŋgi (C.B.) C.21b
Baŋgo (C.B.) D.21
Bangubangu (C.B.) D.27
Basa (C.) A.44
Bati (C.) A.41
Batị (C.B.) C.33
Bea (C.) A.47
Mbede (C.F.) B.21
Ḅemba (C.B., N.R.) M.42a
Bembe (C.B.) D.54
Bembe (A.) H.13
Bena (T.T.) G.64
Bende (T.T.) F.12

Beŋga (R.M.) A.55
Beŋge (C.B.) C.33, C.41
Beo (C.B.) C.42
Mbesa (C.B.) C.51
Mbete (C.F.) B.21
Bila (P.E.) T.23d
Bili (C.B.) D.24
Binji (C.B.) L.22
Bịra (C.B.) D.32
Biisa (N.R.) M.51
Bo- *See also* Bu-
Bo (C.) A.42
Mbo (P.E.) N.32
Mboka (Cabinda, C.B.) H.15
Mboko (C.) A.21
Mbole (C.B.) D.11
Bolo (A.) H.25
Boma (C.F.) B.33
Boma (C.B.) B.42
Bondei (T.T.) G.24
Mboŋge (C.) A.13
Boŋkeŋ (C.) A.42
Mbowe (N.R.) K.32
Bua (C.B.) C.41
Bua, S.E. (C.B.) D.21
Mbuba (C.B.) D.33
Bubaŋgị (C.B.) C.21b
Bụbi (Fernando Po) A.31
Budya (S.R.) T.11d
Mbụdza (C.B.) C.26c

Mbugwe (T.T.) F.34
Buja (C.B.) C.27
Bukala (C.B.) C.61f
Bukoŋgo (C.F.) C.12
Mbuku (C.) A.21
Bukusu (K.) E.31c
Bulịa (C.B.) C.24
Bulu (G.) A.56
Bụlụ (C.) A.62
Bulukị (C.B.) C.26e
Buma (C.B.) B.42
Bumbira (T.T.) E.22g
Mbunda (A., N.R.) K.15
Mbunda, gi- (C.B.) B.48
Mbundu, ki- (A.) H.21
Mbundu, u- (A.) R.11
Mbuŋga (T.T.) P.15
Buŋgili (C.F.) C.11
Buŋgu (T.T.) F.25
Mbunu (C.B.) B.48
Mbunu (C.B.) B.37
Buru (C.B.) C.42
Busoŋo (C.B.) C.83
Buulị (C.B.) C.61e
Buyi (C.B.) D.55
Bvanuma (C.B.) D.33
Bwari (C.B.) D.56
Bwela (C.B.) C.32
Mbwela (A.) K.17
Bwende (C.B.) H.16d
Mbwera (N.R.) L.61

Caga (T.T.) E.62
Cazi (A., N.R.) K.13
Ceŋga (C.) A.41
Cewa (N., N.R.) N.31b
Ch- See C-
Ciga (U.) E.14
Cimba (S.W.) R.31c
Ciokwe, Cioko (A., C.B.) K.11
Cira (G.) B.14
Cokwe (A., C.B.) K.11
Conyi (K.) E.72c
Copi (P.E.) T.31
Cuabo, Cuambo (P.E.) P.34
Cwana (B., S.A., S.R.) S.21

Dabida (K.) E.74a
Dajso (T.T.) E.56
Ndali (T.T.) E.44c
Ndali (T.T.) M.21
Ndamba (T.T.) G.52
Ndandị (C.B.) D.42
Ndau (P.E., S.R.) T.14
Ndebele (S.R.) S.34
Ndeŋgereko (T.T.) P.11
Deŋgese (C.B.) C.81
Digo (K., T.T.) E.73
Dina (C.B.) B.47
Ndiŋgi (Cabinda) H.14
Ndombe (A.) R.12
Ndonde (T.T.) P.24
Ndoŋga (S.W.) R.31
Ndoŋgo (A.) H.21
Dụala (C.) A.24
Dụma, Ndumu (G.) A.72
Dunda (T.T.) G.38
Duruma (K.) E.72d
Dyumba (G.) A.71b
Dzalamo (T.T.) G.33
Ndzali (C.F.) C.16
Dzindza (T.T.) E.23
Dziŋ (C.B.) B.47

Ediya (C.) A.31
Eleku (C.B.) C.26g
Embu (K.) E.52
Ena (C.B.) D.15
Ena (A., N.R.) K.14
Endaŋgabo (T.T.) F.22f
Enya (C.B.) D.15
Eundu, Ewondo (C.) A.61

Faŋ (G., R.M.) A.66
Fiji (T.T.) P.12
Mfinu (C.B.) B.41
Fiote (Cabinda, C.B.) H.16a
Fipa (T.T.) M.13
Foke (C.B.) C.53
Foma (C.B.) C.56
Foto (C.B.) C.26a
Fuliro (C.B.) D.63
Fuluka (C.B.) C.73

Fumu (C.F.) B.31
Fuŋgwe (N.R.) N.21f
Funika, Mfunuŋga (C.B.) B.41

Ŋgala (C.B.) C.26d
Galwa (G.) A.71c
Ganda (U.) E.15a
Ŋgandu (C.B.) C.63
Ŋgazija (Comoro Is.) G.44a
Gbea (C.) A.47
Ŋgelima (C.B.) C.42
Genya (C.B.) D.15
Gikuyu (K.) E.51
Ŋgi̱ndo (T.T.) P.14
Giraŋgo (T.T.) E.44f
Ŋgiri (C.F.) C.11
Giryama (T.T.) E.72a
Gisu (U.) E.31a
Goba (B.) K.33
Gogo (T.T.) G.11
Ŋgola (A.) H.24
Ŋgoli (C.B.) B.46
Ŋgolo (C.) A.11
Ŋgoma (C.B.) M.42b
Ŋgombe (C.B.) C.31
Ŋgomo (G.) A.73
Ŋgoni (T.T.) N.12
Ŋgoni (N.) S.32b
Gova (B.) K.33
Guha (C.B.) D.28
Ŋgulu (T.T.) G.34
Ŋgulu (N., P.E.) P.33
Ŋgulu (C.B.) B.46
Ŋgumba (C.) A.46
Ŋgumbi (R.M.) A.54
Gundi̱ (C.F.) C.14
Guŋgu (U.) E.11
Ŋguŋgulu (C.F.) B.31
Guru (T.T.) G.12, G.35
Ŋguru (T.T.) G.34
Gu̱si̱i̱, Guzii (K.) E.42
Gwamba (P.E., S.A.) T.24
Gweno (T.T.) E.65
Gwere (U.) E.17

Ha (T.T.) D.66

Hadimu (Z.) G.43c
Hai (T.T.) E.62a
Haka (A.) H.25
Hamba (T.T.) E.22b
Hamba (C.B.) D.22
Haŋga (K.) E.32
Haŋgaza (T.T.) D.65
Haŋgiro (T.T.) E.22c
Havu (C.B.) D.52
Haya (T.T.) E.22
Hehe (T.T.) G.63
Hemba (C.B.) L.34
Heŋga (N.) N.21d
Herero (S.W.) R.31a
Hima (R.U.) D.61
Hima (U.) E.13
Hiya (K.) E.32
Hlaŋganu (S.A.) T.23a
Hleŋgwe (P.E., S.R.) T.21a
Horohoro (C.B., T.T.) D.28
Huana (C.B.) H.41
Huku (C.B.) D.33
Humba (A., S.W.) R.21
Hunde (C.B.) D.51
Huɲana (C.B.) H.42
Huŋgu (A.) H.33

I̱ki̱zu̱ (T.T.) E.44g
Ikoma (T.T.) E.45
Ikota (G.) A.74
Ila (N.R.) M.63
Ilamba (T.T.) F.31
Imbi (A.) K.12
Ipaŋga (C.B.) C.61c
Iraŋgi (T.T.) F.33
I̱senyi̱ (T.T.) E.44b
Isubu (C.) A.23
Iwa (N.R.) M.26

Njabi (G.) B.11
Jazi (A.) K.13
Njiem (C.) A.65
Jinja (T.T.) E.23
Jita (T.T.) E.25
Joŋga (P.E.) T.23c
Njuani (Comoro Is.) G.44b

Kabwari (C.B.) D.56
Kagulu (T.T.) G.12
Kahe (T.T.) E.64
Kahonde (C.B.) L.41
Kaka (C.F.) C.13
Kakoŋgo (Cabinda, C.B.) H.16a
Kala (C.B.) C.61f
Kalaŋa (S.R.) T.16
Kamaŋga (N.) N.21b c
Kamba (K.) E.55
Kami (T.T.) G.36
Kande (G.) B.13
Ŋkaŋgala (A.) K.18
Kaŋgana (C.B.) C.26f
Kanyoka (C.B.) L.32
Kaonde (C.B., N.R.) L.41
Karagwe (T.T.) E.21
Karaŋga (S.R.) T.15
Kauma (K.) E.72b
Kela (C.B.) C.75
Kele (G.) A.73
Kele (C.B.) C.55
Ŋkeŋ (C.) A.42
Kerebe (T.T.) E.24
Kete (C.B.) L.21
Kgatla (B.) S.21b
Kikuyu (K.) E.51
Kili (C.B.) C.55
Kimbu (T.T.) F.24
Ḳiŋga (T.T.) G.64
Kioko (A.) K.11
Kiroba (T.T.) E.44f
Kisi (T.T.) G.67
Kisii (K.) E.42
Kisu (U.) E.31b
Kiya (T.T.) F.22c
Koko (C.) A.43
Ŋkole (U.) E.13
Kololo (N.R.) K.31
Kombe (R.M.) A.54
Ŋkomi (G.) A.71c
Komoro (Comoro Is.) G.44
Konde (T.T., N.) M.31
Konde (T.T.) P.23
Koŋgo (C.B.) H.16f
Koŋgo, E. (Cabinda, C.B.) H.16a

Koŋgo, N.E. (C.B.) H.16e
Koŋgo, S. (A., C.B.) H.16g
Koŋgo, Bu- (C.F.) C.12
Koŋgo, tu- (C.B.) C.85
Koŋgola (C.B.) C.72
Konzo, Konjo (C.B., U.) D.41
Korekore (S.R.) T.11b
Koria (K., T.T.) E.43
Kota (C.F.) C.17
Kota (G.) A.74
Kota, W. (C.F.) B.12
Ŋkoya (N.R.) L.62
Kuamba (C.B., U.) D.23
Kuanyama (A., S.W.) R.21
Kuba (C.B.) C.83
Kuba (B.) R.41
Ŋkucu (C.B.) C.73
Kukwe (T.T.) M.31
Kumu (C.B.) D.23
Kunda (N.R., P.E.) N.42
Kundu (C.) A.12
Ŋkụndu (C.B.) C.61b
Kunyi (C.F.) H.12
Kurịa (K., T.T.) E.43
Kusu (K.) E.31c
Kụsụ (C.B.) C.72
Kuta (G.) A.74
Kutu (T.T.) G.37
Ŋkutu (C.B.) C.81
Ŋkụtụ (C.B.) C.73
Kwaŋgwa (N.R.) K.37
Kwaya (T.T.) E.25
Kwese (C.B.) L.13
Kwiri̱ (C.) A.22
Kyopi (U.) E.11

Lala (N.R.) M.52
Lali (C.B.) B.35
Lalịa (C.B.) C.62
Lamba (N.R.) M.54
Lambia (N.R.) N.21h
Laŋge (C.B.) L.31b
Laŋgi̱ (C.) A.53
Laŋgi̱ (T.T.) F.33
Lega (C.B.) D.25
Lega, N.W. (C.B.) D.27

Lega, S.W. (C.B.) D.25
Lele (C.B.) C.84
Lemba (C.B.) C.75
Lembue (C.B.) M.42e
Leŋge (P.E.) T.31
Leŋgola (C.B.) D.12
Lenje (N.R.) M.61
Lesa (C.B.) B.44
Leya (N.R.) M.64c
Liku (C.B.) C.26g
Limba (C.) A.51
Limi (T.T.) F.32
Liŋgi (C.B.) C.32
Loi̧ (C.B.) C.21a
Loki (C.B.) C.26e
Lolia (C.B.) C.62
Lolo (C.B.) C.61a
Lomotua (C.B.) M.42c
Lomwe (P.E.) P.32
Lozi (N.R.) K.21
Luba, E. (C.B.) L.34
Luba, N.E. (C.B.) L.24
Luba, N. (C.B.) L.23
Luba, S. (C.B.) L.33
Luba-Lulua (C.B.) L.31
Luba-Kasai (C.B.) L.31a
Luba-Kataŋga (C.B.) L.33
Lubale (A., N.R.) K.14
Lucazi (A., N.R.) K.13
Lue (C.) A.14
Luena (A., N.R.) K.14
Luimbi (A.) K.12
Lujazi (A., N.R.) K.13
Lulua (C.B.) L.31b
Lumbu (G.) B.16
Lumbu (C.B.) C.54
Luna-Iŋkoŋgo (C.B.) L.23
Lunda (A., C.B., N.R.) L.52
Lundu (C.) A.15
Luŋgu (N.R., T.T.) M.14
Luwunda (C.B.) L.53
Luyana, Luyi (N.R.) K.31

Mabiha (P.E.) P.25
Macame (T.T.) E.62a
Maka (C.) A.64

Make (G.) A.67
Makonde (T.T.) P.23
Makua (P.E.) P.31
Makua, W. (P.E.) P.31
Malila (T.T.) M.24
Mambwe (N.R., T.T.) M.15
Manda (T.T.) N.11
Maŋanja (N.) N.31c
Maŋgala (C.B.) C.26d
Maŋgwato (B.) S.21c
Manyema (C.B.) C.70, D.20, 50
Manyika (P.E., S.R.) T.13a
Maraŋgu (T.T.) E.62b
Maruŋgu (C.B., N.R.) M.41
Masaba (U.) E.31
Maṣi (N.R.) K.34
Mateŋgo (T.T.) N.13
Matu̧mbi (T.T.) P.13
Mavia (P.E.) P.25
Mazaro (P.E.) N.33
Mb- See B-
Meru (K.) E.53
Meru (T.T.) E.61
Mf- See F-
Mihavani (P.E.) P.33
Mi̧tu̧ku̧ (C.B.) D.13
Moŋgo (C.B.) C.61a
Mosi (T.T.) E.62a
Mp- See P-
Mukuni (N.R.) M.61
Mwani (T.T.) E.22h
Mwaŋga (N.R., T.T.) M.22
Mwera (T.T.) P.22
Mweri̧ (T.T.) F.22d
Mv- See V-
Myene (G.) A.71

Naka (C.) A.52
Nano (A.) R.11
Nata (T.T.) E.45
Nc- See C-
Nd- See D-
Ng- See G- or Ŋ-
Nika (K.) E.72
Ni̧lamba (T.T.) F.31
Nj- See J-

Noho, Nohu (C.) A.51
Ns- See S-
Nt- See T-
Nuŋgo (A.) H.36
Ny̨ny̨ (C.B.) C.21c
Nwesi (C.B.) M.42d
Nyabuŋgu (C.B.) D.53
Nyakisaka (T.T.) E.22d
Nyala (U.) E.18
Nyambo (T.T.) E.21
Nyamwaŋga (T.T.) M.22
Nyamwes̨i (T.T.) F.22
Nyaŋga (C.B.) D.43
Nyanja (N.) N.31a
Nyaŋkole (U.) E.13
Nyanyeka (A.) R.13
Nyanyembe (T.T.) F.22a
Nyara (U.) E.18
Nyari (C.B.) D.33
Nyaruanda (R.U.) D.61
Nyaturu (T.T.) F.32
Nyeŋgo (A.) K.17
Nyiha, Nyika (T.T.) M.23
Nyikyy̨sa (T.T., N.R.) M.31
Nyoka (C.B.) L.32
Nyore (K.) E.33
Nyoro (U.) E.11
Nyuli (U.) E.35
Nyuŋgwe (P.E.) N.43
Nz- See Z-

Ɖanja (N.) N.31c
Ɖee (C.B.) B.36
Ɖg- See G-
Ɖhwele (T.T.) G.32
Ɖk- See K-

Oli (C.B.) C.61e

Mpama (C.B.) C.25b
Pande (C.F.) C.15
Paŋga (C.B.) C.61c
Paŋgwa (T.T.) G.64
Paŋgwe (C.) A.66
Pare (T.T.) G.22
Pedi (S.A.) S.22

Pemba (Z.) G.43
Pende (C.B.) L.11
Per̨i, Pere (C.B.) D.32
Mpesa (C.B.) C.26b
Peta (N., N.R.) N.31b
Phemba (Z.) G.43a
Pid̨i (S.A.) S.22
Pimbwe (T.T.) M.11
Pindi (C.B.) L.13
Pindi, Pinji (C.B.) L.11
Pinji (G.) B.13
Podzo (P.E.) N.46
Pogolo (T.T.) G.51
Poka (N.) N.21b
Poke (C.B.) C.53
Ṗokomo (K.) E.71
Ponda (A.) K.13
Mpoŋgwe (G.) A.71a
Poto (C.B.) C.26a
Mpoto (T.T.) N.14
Mpovi (G.) B.13
Ṗuki (C.B.) C.53
Puku (R.M.) A.52
Mpukusu (A.) K.33
Mpuŋgwe (G.) A.71a
Punu (G.) B.15
Putsu (P.E.) T.26

R- See also L-
Rabai (T.T.) E.72e
Ragoli (K.) E.41
Rebu (C.B.) C.21b
Rega (C.B.) D.25
Mrima (T.T.) G.42c
Rim̨i (T.T.) F.32
Roloŋ (B.) S.21a
Rombi (C.) A.13
Rombo (T.T.) E.62c
Rondo (C.) A.15
Roŋga (P.E., S.A.) T.24
Rori (T.T.) G.61
Rotse (N.R.) K.31
Ruanda (R.U.) D.61
Rue (P.E., S.R.) N.45
Rufiji (T.T.) P.12
Ruguru (T.T.) G.35

Ruihi (T.T.) P.12
Rumbu (C.B.) C.54
Rundi (R.U.) D.62
Rungu (G.) A.71b
Rungu (T.T., N.R.) M.14
Rungu (C.B., N.R.) M.41
Rungwa (T.T.) M.12
Rusa (T.T.) E.63
Rwo (T.T.) E.61

Saamia (U.) E.34
Safwa (T.T.) M.25
Sagala (K.) E.74b
Sagala (T.T.) G.39
Sagara, N. (T.T.) G.12
Sakata (C.B.) B.44
Sake (G.) A.74
Salampasu (C.B.) L.51
Sama (A.) H.23
Samba (C.B.) L.12
Sambaa, Sambara (T.T.) G.23
Sanga (C.B.) L.35
Sangaan (P.E., S.A.) T.23a
Sango (T.T.) G.61
Sango (G.) B.14
Sangwe (S.R.) T.11a
Sanjo (N.R.) K.36
Saraka (K.) E.54
Sasi (T.T.) F.21
Seba (N.R.) M.55
Sebo (G.) B.12
Seke (G.) A.56
Sena (P.E.) N.44
Senga (N.R.) N.21d
Nsenga (N.R.) N.41
Sengele (C.B.) C.22
Sengeju (T.T.) E.56
Sengo (C.B.) C.26
Sese (U.) E.15b
Sese (C.B.) D.32
Sh- *is written* S- *and indexed as* S-
Siki (C.) A.45
Sila (C.B., N.R.) M.41b
Silele (C.B.) C.84
Simaa (N.R.) K.35
Simbiti (T.T.) E.44k

Sinji (A.) H.36
Siora (T.T.) E.44d
Sira (G.) B.14
Siska (N.) N.15
So (C.B.) C.52
Sofala (S.R., P.E.) T.14
Soga (U.) E.16
Sokili (T.T.) M.31
Soko (C.B.) C.52
Soli (N.R.) M.62
Sona (S.R.) T.11-15
Songe (C.B.) L.23
Songo (A.) H.26
Songola (C.B.) D.24
Songomeno (C.B.) C.82
Sonjo, Sonyo (T.T.) E.46
Sono (C.B.) C.83
Su (C.B.) D.42
Subi (T.T.) D.64
Subia (B.) K.42
Subu (C.) A.23
Suku (C.B.) H.32
Sukulumbwe (N.R.) M.63
Sukuma (T.T.) F.21
Sumburu (C.B.) D.32
Sumbwa (T.T.) F.23
Sundi (C.B.) H.16c
Sungu (C.B.) C.71
Suthu (S.A.) S.23
Sutu (T.T.) N.13
Swahili (K., T.T., Z.) G.42
Swaka (N.R.) M.53
Swazi (Swaziland) S.33a
Sweta (T.T.) E.44e

Tabara (S.R.) T.11c
Taabwa (C.B., N.R.) M.41a
Taita (K.) E.74
Taveta (T.T.) G.21
Tebe (P.E.) T.13b
Tebele (S.R.) S.34
Tege (C.F.) B.32
Teke, E. (C.F.) B.31
Teke, N. (C.F.) B.23
Teke, N.E. (C.F.) B.21
Teke, S. (C.B.) B.37

Teke, S.W. (C.F., C.B.) B.35
Teke, W. (C.F.) B.32
Tembo (A.) H.34
Tembo (N.R.) M.27
Tende (C.B.) B.43
Teŋgo (T.T.) N.13
Tete (C.B.) B.44
Tete (P.E.) N.43
Tetela (C.B.) C.71
Th- (for θ-) see Ṣ-
Thoŋga (P.E.) T.23
Tiene (C.B.) B.43
Tikulu (K.) G.41
Tio (C.F., C.B.) B.35
Ṭiṭu̱ (C.B.) C.61d
Toka (N.R.) M.64b
Tomba (C.B.) C.25
Toŋga (N.R., S.R.) M.64a
Toŋga (N.) N.15
Toŋga (P.E.) T.32
Toŋgwe (T.T.) F.11
Topoke (C.B.) C.53
Toro (U.) E.12
Totela (N.R.) K.41
Tsaya (C.F.) B.23
Tsh- See C-
Tsogo (G.) B.13
Tsoŋga (P.E., S.A.) T.23b
Tsotso (K.) E.32b
Tswa (P.E.) T.21b
Tswana (B., S.A., S.R.) S.21
Tu̱beta (T.T.) G.21
Tukoŋgo (C.B.) C.85
Tuku (C.B.) D.13
Ntum (C.) A.63
Tu̱mba (C.B.) C.23
Ntumba (C.B.) C.25
Tumbatu (Z.) G.44
Tumbi (T.T.) P.13
Tumbuka (N.) N.21a
Tuŋgu (C.B.) C.42
Turu (T.T.) F.32
Turumbu (C.B.) C.54
Tusi (R.U., T.T.) D.61, 66

Ulị (C.B.) C.61e

Unda (C.B.) L.53
Unguja (Z.) G.42d

Mvela (C.) A.44
Venda (S.A., S.R.) S.11
Vili (C.F.) H.11
Vinza (T.T.) D.57
Mvita (K.) G.42b

Wanda, Wandia (T.T.) M.21
Wandia (N.R.) N.21k
Waŋga (K.) E.32a
Waŋgata (C.B.) C.25b
Wanji (T.T.) G.66
Wemba (N.R.) M.42
Wenya (N.R.) N.21g
Wisa (N.R.) M.51
Woŋgo (C.B.) C.85
Wumu, Wumbu (C.B.) B.37
Wuŋgu (T.T.) F.25
Wunjo (T.T.) E.62b
Wuri (C.) A.24

Xhosa, Xosa (S.A.) S.31

Yailịma (C.B.) C.61g
Yaka (G.) B.34
Yaka (C.B.) H.31
Yaka (C.F.) C.13
Yaŋga (C.F.) C.13
Yanzi (C.B.) B.45
Yanzi (C.B.) C.21, B.26
Yao (T.T., P.E., N.) P.21
Yau̱nde (C.) A.61
Yeei (B.) R.41
Yela (C.B.) C.74
Yembe (C.B.) L.24
Yeye (B.) R.41
Yombe (C.B.) H.16b
Yombe (N.R.) N.21e
Yoŋgo (A.) H.35b
Yoza (T.T.) E.22e

Nzabi (G.) B.11
Zanakị (T.T.) E.44a
Zaramo (T.T.) G.33

Nzelị (C.F.) C.16
Zezuru (S.R.) T.12
Ziba (T.T.) E.22a
Zịmba (C.B.) D.26
Zimba (C.B.) D.15
Zịmu (C.) A.65
Zinza (T.T.) E.23
Zombo (A.) H.16h
Nzuani (Comoro Is.) G.44b
Zulu (S.A.) S.32

BANTU WORD DIVISION
A New Study of an Old Problem

MALCOLM GUTHRIE

LONDON AND NEW YORK

First published in 1948 by Oxford University Press

This edition first published in 2018
by Routledge
2 Park Square, Milton Park, Abingdon, Oxon OX14 4RN

and by Routledge
711 Third Avenue, New York, NY 10017

Routledge is an imprint of the Taylor & Francis Group, an informa business

© 1948 International African Institute 1948

All rights reserved. No part of this book may be reprinted or reproduced or utilised in any form or by any electronic, mechanical, or other means, now known or hereafter invented, including photocopying and recording, or in any information storage or retrieval system, without permission in writing from the publishers.

Trademark notice: Product or corporate names may be trademarks or registered trademarks, and are used only for identification and explanation without intent to infringe.

British Library Cataloguing-in-Publication Data
A catalogue record for this book is available from the British Library

ISBN: 978-1-138-08975-4 (Set)
ISBN: 978-1-315-10381-5 (Set) (ebk)
ISBN: 978-1-138-09582-3 (Volume 11) (hbk)
ISBN: 978-1-138-09585-4 (Volume 11) (pbk)
ISBN: 978-1-315-10553-6 (Volume 11) (ebk)

Publisher's Note
The publisher has gone to great lengths to ensure the quality of this reprint but points out that some imperfections in the original copies may be apparent.

Disclaimer
The publisher has made every effort to trace copyright holders and would welcome correspondence from those they have been unable to trace.

INTERNATIONAL AFRICAN INSTITUTE
MEMORANDUM XXII

BANTU WORD DIVISION

A New Study of an Old Problem

By

MALCOLM GUTHRIE, Ph.D., B.Sc.

Published for the
INTERNATIONAL AFRICAN INSTITUTE
by the
OXFORD UNIVERSITY PRESS
LONDON   NEW YORK   TORONTO
1948

*This paper has been published with the
assistance of a subsidy from* THE SCHOOL
OF ORIENTAL AND AFRICAN STUDIES
UNIVERSITY OF LONDON

PRINTED IN GREAT BRITAIN
AT THE UNIVERSITY PRESS, OXFORD
BY CHARLES BATEY, PRINTER TO THE UNIVERSITY

AUTHOR'S ACKNOWLEDGEMENT

THIS study deals with a question that has been the subject of protracted controversy. For this if for no other reason I should like to express my appreciation of the readiness of the International African Institute to publish it as a Memorandum. Naturally the opinions expressed are my own, and the issue of the paper in this form does not mean that it represents the views of the Institute.

My thanks are also due to the School of Oriental and African Studies for their willingness to make a grant towards the cost of publication.

MALCOLM GUTHRIE

SCHOOL OF ORIENTAL AND
AFRICAN STUDIES
UNIVERSITY OF LONDON
1948

BANTU WORD DIVISION

NEARLY all the earliest writers on Bantu languages used the system of word division which appeared to them to be the most natural, consequently few of them thought it necessary even to explain the reasons that had influenced them in developing such a system. Before long, however, it became clear that quite different types of word division were being practised, sometimes for one and the same language. There can be little doubt that this situation has given rise to more disagreement among workers in Bantu languages than any other single problem. Broadly speaking there have been two different opinions, known as the conjunctivist and the disjunctivist; and the fact that these two points of view are irreconcilable has led to much arguing, which has all too often proved fruitless. To-day the general tendency is unquestionably more and more towards a conjunctivist system, but there are still so many convinced disjunctivists that the matter can hardly be said to have been settled. It is not the purpose of this present paper to add one more voice to the general clamour. On the contrary the question of word division will be discussed from a somewhat different angle, with the intention of discovering a way of solving the problem that may be more conclusive. In the opinion of the writer most of the difficulties can be resolved in such a way as to admit of one solution only.

At the outset it may be desirable to determine the precise nature of the problem we are discussing. The view taken in this study is that there is an inherent weakness in the attitudes represented by the very terms conjunctivist and disjunctivist. The reader will therefore not be startled by the assertion that the present writer does not associate himself with either of them. It seems fairly certain that the inconclusiveness of much of the discussion about word division has arisen through approaching the problem from the wrong end. What has been called the problem of word division has in fact been treated as a problem of 'word-fusion'. It has usually been tacitly assumed that there are certain fundamental parts of speech, such as nouns and verbs, and so all that has to be decided is whether or not any other smaller pieces are to be joined on to them. But this is surely begging the question, and we may well ask what grounds there are for such assumptions. The crux of the matter is how the so-called nouns and verbs are to be identified. In most cases it is found that certain words in a Bantu language are termed nouns because they seem to be equivalent to things that have been called nouns in English or some other European language, and so on. But this is merely arbitrating the problems of Bantu languages by reference to the traditional treatment of European languages. We must surely begin with the facts of the language in question, and the most fundamental of these facts is the sentence, not some theoretical 'parts of speech'. The real problem then is: Where ought the sentence to be divided? This is quite different from the usual question: To join or not to join?, which has produced the conjunctivist who believes in much joining, and the disjunctivist who does not.

Putting it more clearly, what we want to know is where there are going to be breaks in the sentence, at which the writer will lift his pen and the printer will put a space. In speech many sentences are fully 'conjunctive', since they are heard as an unbroken stream. However, to write a language in unbroken sentences would not only make reading almost impossible, but would also obscure the structure of the language; so we have to discover the best way of chopping up the sentence. It is for this reason that this study claims to be outside the usual conjunctive-disjunctive discussion, since it commences with what is already joined, and so is not concerned with questions about whether or not to join up certain elements. What has to be done is to show adequate reasons for every break which is made in the sentence.

From this it follows that for our purpose there is no value in the usual method of building up 'words' until it is decided that the limit has been reached. Moreover, it will most probably be begging the question to use phonetic criteria to determine what is or is not a word. One result of the approach used in this paper is that we must assert that a given part of the sentence displays certain phonetic characteristics just because it is a word, and not that it is a word because of these characteristics. If, in a language like Swahili, after the words have been established it is found that these have penultimate stress, then such stress must be taken as a sign of the approaching end of the word. Such a fact may then be used as a quick practical means of determining word-limits, but it would be a misrepresentation to say that the stress makes the word. Similarly, if in a language like Bemba it is found that a syllable containing a long vowel is never the last in a word, this is because it occurs immediately before a break in the sentence, and not vice versa. Moreover, if it be argued, as has been done, that a given part of a sentence is a word because it displays certain phonetic characteristics, what is to be done in the case of another language that has an almost identical grammatical structure but different phonetic features? If on the contrary the limits of the words can be determined on other grounds, then it will be possible to make observations on the phonetic behaviour of the individual words in any given language.

The use of a different approach means that little or no specific reference will be needed to the various contributions that have been made to the discussions on word division. Nevertheless, there is one statement made by Junod in his *Ronga Grammar*[1] which expresses so neatly a common confusion in terms that it cannot be passed over. He claims that in following a disjunctive system he is actually using a 'grammatical' approach. It is, however, clear from his own words that by 'grammatical' he really means 'notional'. Because in Ronga the element **-ta-**, which indicates the 'future' is similar in shape[2] to **-ta-** which *means* 'come', therefore he claims it is a separate word, and asserts that **ndi-ta-bona** 'I shall see' really is 'I come to see'. But this is not a grammatical attitude at all. It is just another example of the common failure to realize that grammar is not primarily concerned with ideas 'inherent' in words or elements, but with the behaviour of this or that part of the sentence within the structure of the language. There is no space here to give examples to show the chaos that would result in Bantu or other languages from a consistent application of the notional principle in word division.

In this study the technique of investigation used is grammatical in the sense just

[1] *Grammaire Ronga*, 1896, by H. A. Junod. The following relevant passages occur on page 41, the italics being his: 'Les uns (les Anglais) tenant compte uniquement de l'accentuation, réunissent en un seul mot tous les *ensembles de mots* qui n'ont qu'un seul accent.' 'D'autres grammairiens tenant compte plutôt de la valeur grammaticale des mots, les séparent selon leur sens propre, indépendamment de la question de leur accentuation, comme on le fait du reste, pour les langues européennes. C'est la *méthode analytique* et grammaticale.'

[2] We use the term 'shape' to refer simply to the sounds of which any part of the sentence is composed. Those which have the same shape are therefore homophones.

indicated. The only way to decide where the sentence is to be broken is to treat the whole subject from the point of view of syntax and morphology. The paper is divided into three main parts. The first deals with the most important ways in which such an investigation may be undertaken, the illustrations being drawn from more than one language. In the second part the technique established is applied to one particular language, while in the third the phonetic behaviour of the broken sentence is observed in some detail.

Terminology and Spelling

In order to facilitate the development of our thesis we need to have some simple terms to refer to the facts we are handling. The parts into which the sentence is ultimately broken up will be termed *Distinct Pieces*, or more simply *Pieces*.[1] The distinct piece will then occupy the place occupied by the *word* in conventional grammar, and we shall speak of one-piece or two-piece sentences and so on. The points in the sentence which mark the limits of the distinct pieces will be termed *Breaks*. From this it follows that each distinct piece is delimited by a break at either end. The beginning and end of the sentence will therefore always be regarded as breaks. Any point in the sentence which is being examined will be referred to by the accepted term *Junction*,[1] so the purpose of this study may be described as merely determining which junctions are breaks. In addition, the usual term *Element* will be reserved for the smaller parts of the sentence, especially those which operate the grammatical processes of the language. In order to enable the investigation to be conducted without presuppositions, a special *ad hoc* term is required to refer to any part of the sentence which is being examined experimentally, and for this *Segment* will be used. This term is adopted in order that its use may give no indication as to whether or not the part of the sentence under discussion is likely to be a distinct piece. The term 'segment' has no permanent value, since it will no longer be needed when it has been decided which segments are distinct pieces.

It is difficult to know what is the best way of spelling the examples cited in the course of the study. It would be unsatisfactory merely to use the conventional system, since this would frequently distract the reader's attention from the point at issue. On the other hand, if the accepted spelling is modified, it may appear like an attempt to prejudge the question. As an expedient therefore, the examples given in the first part will be written in the words of the accepted system, but they will all be linked up with hyphens; this latter device is intended to emphasize the importance of the sentence as an entity. In the second part of the paper a different method is employed, and this is explained there.

I

THE TECHNIQUE OF SENTENCE DIVISION

There are several principles which may be invoked in a discussion on the division of the sentence. Since all of these principles are not equally valid, they must be examined to see which of them may be used with safety.

[1] The terms 'piece' and 'junction' are both due to S. Yoshitake; see his article entitled 'A New Classification of the Constituents of Spoken Japanese', in the *Bulletin of the School of Oriental and African Studies*, vol. viii, Part IV.

It is important to observe one fact about any of the tests that may be applied in this way. This is that the validity of any test does not necessarily involve the validity of its converse. Thus suppose for example we test whether or not it is possible to insert something at a given junction. If it should be found that something can be inserted, this may under certain conditions be accepted as evidence that there is a break at this junction. It would not, however, automatically follow that there is no break at another junction, where under similar conditions nothing can be inserted. The converse would have to be considered on its own merits, without direct reference to the original principle. Failure to observe this might easily lead to false conclusions.

(a) Isolation

One of the most obvious ways of attempting to discover the breaks in a sentence is the experimental isolation of different segments. There can be little doubt that some such idea underlies much of the usual discussion about word division. Thus for example in the Swahili sentence, **amesoma-kitabu** 'he has read the book', there is felt to be a break at the hyphen because it is equally possible to say **amesoma** 'he has read', while **kitabu** is the 'name' for a book.

Now there are several difficulties in this kind of argument. When it is said that a segment can be isolated, what is really meant is that it is 'stable', i.e. that it is capable of standing by itself as a complete sentence without any other word. When we attempt to apply the principle of isolation, we find that there are not many kinds of stable segments. Moreover, while it is true that **amesoma** happens to be stable, it by no means follows that there is a break at the hyphen. If it could be shown that **kitabu** were equally stable, then we might be forced to conclude that the sentence has at least two pieces, but there appears to be no means of proving that **kitabu** is stable. The fact of its duty[1] in naming a book is really not relevant to our problem. It is true that in reply to such a question as 'What is this?' the normal reply would be **kitabu** 'a book'; but the significant thing is that this can quite well be replaced by **ni-kitabu** 'it is a book', whereas the apparently similar segment in our sentence cannot.

There is continually the difficulty of establishing the identity or the distinctiveness of a particular sentence with respect to a segment of another sentence when they happen to be similar in shape. In some cases it is immediately clear that there is no identity, e.g. in Swahili, **piga** 'strike!' happens to be similar to the last part of **amekwisha-piga** 'he has struck'. That they are quite different things can be shown by contrasting their behaviour in junction with the element **wa**, e.g. **wapige** 'strike them!', **amekwisha-wapiga** 'he has struck them'. In other cases, however, it is not so easy to be sure that the two segments are distinct. For example, in Kongo, **túásalaŋga**[2] 'we were working' has a segment which is similar in shape to **túásala** 'we worked'. Does this mean that there is a break before **-ŋga**, since it is difficult to prove that the two segments **túásala** are not the same thing? The direct appeal

---

[1] 'Duty' is concerned with meaning and notion, and is used where some writers speak of 'function', since this latter term is given a more specialized meaning. Thus it is permissible to speak of the 'naming duty' of some segments, or the 'adverbial duty' of others.

[2] With the exception of Swahili, all the languages from which examples are taken are tonal. In the marking of the tones an acute accent on the vowel denotes a syllable with a high-tone, an upright accent one with a mid-tone, while the absence of an accent indicates the lower level of tone.

to grammatical behaviour will be dealt with in a later section, but for the moment the important thing is that even if it is possible to find a stable segment that has the same shape as the one we are studying, nothing can be inferred from this fact unless the identity of the two can be proved.

The converse of the principle of isolation is completely inapplicable, since we can never assert that a given segment is not a distinct piece merely because it is not stable. Thus though the segment ŋga- in the Bemba sentence ŋga-bámbí-bááyísá is never stable, there are other reasons why it has to be treated as a distinct piece.

(b) Interpolation or Omission

Another method which at first sight seems easy to apply consists in experimentally inserting or removing segments within a sentence. The inference might then be made that wherever a segment can be inserted there is a break, e.g. in Swahili, **alifika-jana** 'he arrived yesterday', **alifika-mjini-jana** 'he arrived at the village yesterday'. The fact that **mjini** can be inserted at the hyphen in the first sentence might appear to prove that there is a break there.

That such a conclusion may be false will be seen from the following two Bemba sentences, **akábuela-kúnó**[1] 'he will return from here', **akábuelela-kúnó** 'he will return to here'. If the principle of interpolation and omission were universally applicable, then the presence of the segment **-el-** in the second sentence should prove that there is a break at the point where it is inserted. The fallacy of this argument is that it can be shown that **-el-** is not a distinct piece, and so is not really interpolated. In fact the presence of **-el-** is due to a morphological process, as can be shown in other ways. We must therefore insist that interpolation can never be a valid test unless the inserted segment can itself be shown to be a distinct piece on other grounds.

A second reservation must also be made with respect to the use of this method. It may frequently merely beg the question through insufficient attention being given to the grammatical structure of the sentence. For example, in the Swahili sentence, **ni-visu-vya-watoto** 'they are the children's knives', it would not be conclusive that there must be a break at the third hyphen since the distinct piece **wale** can be inserted there, as in **ni-visu-vya-wale-watoto** 'they are the knives of those children'. Suppose that there is no break after **-vya-** in either case, then the two sentences could each contain a similar type of distinct piece, **vyawatoto** and **vyawale** respectively. In other words, the possibility of inserting a distinct piece like **wale** at that particular junction proves nothing either way. This means that the principle of interpolation may be of small value in deciding where the breaks occur in a sentence.

A further example of the inconclusiveness of this test may be found in languages like Kongo, where an element **-ko** is found at the end of many negative sentences. For example, there are these two sentences, **ka-túásumba-muínda-ko** 'we did not buy a lamp', **ka-túásumba-muínda-anéne-ko** 'we did not buy a large lamp'. The fact that a segment like **-anéne-** can be interpolated after **-muínda-** proves nothing, unless we have some other means of finding out the grammatical relationship between **-ko** and what precedes it. It might be that this element is a distinct piece, or it might

---

[1] In this language there is considerable discrepancy between the pronunciation of the tones according as they occur at the end of the sentence or not. The tones as marked in the examples take no account of this fact.

be that it forms one piece with what precedes, in which case the final piece in the two sentences could be **muíndako** and **anéneko** respectively.

The converse of the principle of omission is much more useful for our purpose. We frequently find a certain kind of element in a language, which is always in junction with one of another series of elements that can never be omitted. Under such conditions very strong reasons would have to be adduced to prove that a break occurs at such a junction. For example, in the Swahili sentence, **watoto-wamefika** 'the children have arrived', the segment **watoto** may be omitted, but the **-wa-** in **-wamefika** could not be. The rule simply is that **-me-** must always be preceded by **wa-** or some other member of the series to which it belongs. This means the junction between **-wa-** and **-me-** is of a kind quite different from that between **watoto-** and **-wamefika**, and that quite probably the latter is a break but the former is not.

(c) Substitution

In many respects this method of dealing with the problem of sentence dissection is merely an extension of the principle of interpolation just considered. Since, however, it is one that might be used, it must be examined.

In applying the principle the greatest difficulty is in knowing what is being replaced. For example, if we compare the two Bemba sentences, **icísóté-náacílubá** 'the hat is lost', and **icílolá-náacílubá** 'the mirror is lost', does the fact of the substitution establish a break at the hyphen? If so, then is there also a break after **icí-**? Until we are able to decide whether the substitution is **icísóté/icílolá** or only **sóté/lolá**, which is a purely grammatical question, the value of substitution as a means of finding the breaks in such sentences is very small.

A still greater difficulty is that the mere substitution of segments without the application of other tests merely divides up the sentence into its morphological elements, and that has no real bearing on our present investigation. Thus the Bemba **tuáfíká** 'we have just arrived' would appear as **tu á fík á** since it is possible to replace each of these four segments with other comparable ones.

There is some value in the principle of substitution in certain cases when it is applied under controlled grammatical conditions. If a given segment of a sentence can be replaced by another which can be shown to be at once a distinct piece and grammatically similar, then there are strong reasons for regarding such a segment as a distinct piece too. For example, in the Swahili sentence, **visu-vya-mgeni-ni-vikubwa** 'the knives of the stranger are big ones', the segment **-vya-mgeni-** can be replaced by **-vyake-**, as in **visu-vyake-ni-vikubwa** 'his knives are big ones'. If, therefore, it is found that **vyake** is a distinct piece, **vyamgeni** is almost certainly one too.

(d) Interruption

An interesting test to apply in the search for the breaks in the sentence is that of interruption. This consists in finding those junctions at which the sentence may be completely or partially interrupted. It frequently happens that segments that are not stable may be found interrupted, as in the Bemba sentence, **leeló-cínó-cíísumá** 'but this is a good one'. Here an interruption may occur after **-cínó-**, the sentence then being completed afterwards, and this fact may be taken to show that there is a break at this junction, even in those cases where the interruption is not actually made.

It is open to question whether this is an infallible test, since situations do arise in which interruption occurs at a junction which can be shown in other ways not to be a break. An example of this occurs in Bemba when a hearer mis-hears a sentence like **kúlí-ífipúná** 'there are stools', thinking he heard **kúlí-ícipúná** 'there is a stool'. When the speaker realizes the mistake he may say **nsítíilé-íci-ntiilé-ífi** 'I did not say "ici" I said "ifi"', in which the tones of the segments **-íci-** and **-ífi** show them to be interrupted fragments of **ícipúná** and **ífipúná** respectively. In some languages there is another type of interruption which can scarcely be a sign of a break. Here is an example from Mangala, where a speaker may say in certain situations, **asómbí-mikandá-mí-** 'he has bought books ...', holding up three fingers as he does so; his hearers then say **-sáto**, which is presumably the rest of the interrupted segment **-mísáto** 'three'.

In fixed formulae interruption is very common, and may under these special conditions provide a safe criterion for the placing of breaks. In Bemba, for example, there is usually a complete interruption of the following formula at the second hyphen, **ciaŋga-ukúlílá-ní-pá-lúpákó** 'when the bush-baby cries it is in the tree-hollow'. It is then at the option of the hearer whether or not he completes the formula. On the other hand, it should be noted that the general rules for word division frequently do not operate with respect to such fixed formulae, so they really fall outside the scope of this present study, e.g. **ní-buu-ciaŋga-ukulila** 'it is the way the bush-baby cries'. There are good reasons for regarding such a sentence as consisting of one distinct piece only, in spite of the fact that in current Bemba a segment like **ukulila** is itself a distinct piece.

(e) Transposition

Sometimes the order of the segments in a sentence can be changed without modifying its grammatical structure. When this is possible we may be provided with some useful indications on the place of the breaks. For example, the Swahili sentence, **watoto-wamefika** 'the children have arrived', may be transposed to **wamefika-watoto** without disturbing the relationship between the two main segments. Since then the segment **watoto** commences with a break in the first sentence and ends with a break in the second, it is reasonable to conclude that there is a break at each end in both cases. A similar argument could be followed for **wamefika**, but this would lead to an identical conclusion: that in both sentences there is a break at the hyphen. Another example of the application of the principle of transposition may be given from Bemba, where **ŋga-bámbí-bááyísá** 'if the others come' can be transposed to **bámbí-ŋga-bááyísá**. From this it may be inferred that there is a break at each of the hyphens.

If transposition involves a modification of the grammatical relationships, a different sentence results, and this invalidates any comparison for our present purpose. The following two sentences from Swahili provide an example of this sort of thing: (a) **mtoto-ameleta-vitabu-vyake** 'the child has brought his books', (b) **ameleta-vitabu-vyake-mtoto** 'he has brought the *child's* books'. In (a) there is a clear relationship between **mtoto-** and **-ameleta-**; in (b), on the other hand, **-mtoto** is not in relationship with **ameleta-**, since if **-watoto** is used in place of **-mtoto** the only necessary change is in **-vyake-** which must be replaced by **-vyao-**, as (c) **ameleta-**

vitabu-vyao-watoto 'he has brought the *children's* books'. If, on the other hand, **watoto-** is used in place of **mtoto-** in (*a*) it is impossible to retain **-ameleta-**, instead we get (*d*) **watoto-wameleta-vitabu-vyake** 'the children have brought his books'. It is clear then that the transposition of **mtoto** has in fact revealed nothing that its simple omission would not, since its grammatical relationships are not the same in the two cases.

(*f*) *Function*

Most of the principles that have been studied up to this point are concerned with what might be called the 'grammar of movement', but there remains the very important 'grammar of relationships' to be considered. For this purpose the term 'function' is used in a specialized sense, and, as has already been indicated in a footnote, it must be clearly distinguished from 'duty'. The function of any segment, in the sense in which it is being used here, is concerned solely with the syntagmatic (i.e. syntactical and morphological) relationships into which it has entered or could enter.

As will be shown in Part II, the appeal to function is one of the most important ways of seeking a solution to the problem of sentence division. This means that when we experiment with any segment, the most significant thing about it is the nature of its capacity for syntagmatic relations, together with the reasons for this capacity in so far as they may be discovered.

In the last resort it is only by determining the function of a segment that it can be identified. Thus if we find two segments that are homophonous, we do not know whether they are similar or even comparable until we determine their respective functions. Any conclusions based on an accidental similarity of shape may well be false, a possibility that can be avoided by establishing the function of the segments in question. Even similarity in meaning is an unsafe guide in identifying segments, since by 'meaning' is usually meant an appeal to the usage of the equivalent in some European language. The significance of this in our present study is that until we are in a position to identify a segment, it is scarcely possible to discuss whether or not it is a distinct piece.

An illustration of one of the simpler appeals to function may be seen in the following two sentences from Bemba: (*a*) **nsitílé-uyú-mufúkó** 'I have bought *this* sack', (*b*) **nsitílé-akámufúkó** 'I have bought a small sack'. The final segment **-mufúkó** has the same shape in both sentences, and in both cases its meaning is something to do with 'sack', but this does not mean that the two segments are identical. In fact the contrary can be proved by the following test. In (*a*) **-mufúkó** can be followed by **-úákúé** 'his' in close grammatical relationship with it, but the similar segment in (*b*) cannot, a fact which can be shown to distinguish the two segments. So in spite of the similarity in shape and 'meaning', these two segments are distinct things and any argument from one to the other in fixing breaks would be fallacious.

In the next part of this paper then the question of word division will be studied chiefly by reference to the function of the segments. Where necessary and possible, judicious use will also be made of those other principles that have been established, either to supplement or to confirm decisions reached from a consideration of grammatical behaviour and potentialities.

II

Dividing the Sentences in a Bantu Language

To undertake an investigation of this kind satisfactorily it is clearly necessary to confine our attention to one particular language. The language chosen for this purpose is Bemba, a choice dictated by two main considerations. The first of these concerns the grammatical structure of the language, which happens to be unusually complicated and to contain most of the features that are important for our study. The second is that we have adequate data about its pronunciation, while the rules governing the pronunciation are sufficiently complex to enable interesting observations to be made in Part III on the phonetic behaviour of the distinct pieces.

Since the discussion is primarily grammatical it will be necessary to use some grammatical terms. During the investigation then we shall speak of 'nominal segment' and 'verbal segment'. Within the limits of this paper it is not possible to explain these terms, nor to give the criteria that determine into which of the two categories any given segment has to be placed. After the distinct pieces have been established we shall refer simply to 'nominals' and 'verbals'.

In order not to prejudge the question by the spelling of the segments, a purely syllabic division will be used, without any reference to conventional systems. The syllables will all be separated by hyphens, and though this may make the identity of the sentences difficult to detect at first, it has the advantage of keeping much nearer to the fact of the unbroken sentence. The actual orthography differs slightly from that commonly used for the language, since it is desirable to keep as far as possible to the phonological structure. Thus, for example, vowels are written uncoalesced, as in **a-ká-i-sa** 'he will come' (pronounced *akéésa*) where **-ka-** is identifiable as a grammatical element. Also the special pronunciation of **-s-** in junction with **-i-** will not be shown, as in **tu-a-pu-sí-lé** 'we missed' (pronounced *twaapuʃílé*), cf. **tu-á-pú-sá** 'we have just missed' (pronounced *twáápúsá*).

In order to simplify the spelling as rapidly as possible, a hyphen will be dispensed with at any given point as soon as it has been shown that there is no break there.

1. Nominal Segments

To facilitate our study, nominal segments are classified according to their behaviour within the system of grammatical agreement that is so characteristic of Bantu languages. We shall refer to those parts of the sentence which operate the system as 'concordial elements', and there will be two kinds of such elements. There is the independent element, which is the sign of a segment that controls an agreement, and the dependent element, which is the sign of a segment that is agreeing with another. Nominal segments are therefore classified according to the number and nature of their concordial elements.

(1) *Segments with One Concordial Element*

Under this heading we have to consider some of the most important types of segment in the language, such as those in (*a*) **í-ci-sí-ma-cíi-tá-lí** 'the well is a deep one', (*b*) **cíi-sí-ma-cí-mbí** 'it is another well'. It may be quickly discovered that the segment **cíi-sí-ma-** in (b) is stable, whereas the somewhat similar one **í-ci-sí-ma-** in (a) is not. We shall study the unstable kind first, and consider sentence (a). Using the test of transposition, we find that there are similar grammatical relationships in **cíi-tá-lí-í-ci-sí-ma**, and therefore may conclude that the sentence contains at least two distinct pieces. With this one break then we have (a) **í-ci-sí-ma cíi-tá-lí**.

The next problem is whether or not there are any breaks in **í-ci-sí-ma**. If we take the last two syllables, we find that they can never be transposed, omitted, or substituted, neither can anything ever be interpolated between them. For these reasons we clearly have to regard **-sí-ma** as an indivisible unit; there will therefore be no need to separate into syllables this or similar segments. What then about the junction immediately before **-síma**? One fact to be considered is that **-síma** never occurs unless it is preceded by **-ci-** or some other element, such as **-fi-**, which is a member of the same series as **-ci-**. The presumption then is that there is no break at this point. There is, however, a further argument based on the grammatical behaviour of the segments, and since this is one which is relevant to other parts of our investigation, it must be considered in some detail.

Suppose we take the two sentences, (c) **í-ci-sé-le cíi-tá-lí** 'the sandbank is a long one', (d) **ú-mu-sé-le úu-tá-lí** 'the wicker-plate is a long one'. In (c) the segment **í-ci-sé-le** controls the agreement **cíi-** in **cíi-tá-lí**, while in (d) **ú-mu-sé-le** controls the distinct agreement **úu-** in **úu-tá-lí**. This then is simply a kind of grammatical gender, operating by means of initial elements; the two segments belong to different genders so we shall call them gender X and gender Y respectively for the sake of our present argument. The important question that must be decided is what exactly it is that belongs to this or that gender. Is it the small segment **-séle**, or is it the longer segment **í-ci-séle** that belongs to gender X? If we say that it is **-séle**, then we are faced with a situation in which a segment contains no sign in itself of the gender to which it belongs. In fact we should have to identify **-séle** in (c) with the similar segment in (d), merely saying that in gender X it means 'sandbank' and in gender Y 'wicker-plate'. Such an attitude would, however, surely be putting the effect for the cause, as may be shown by considering the operation of grammatical gender in other languages.

In French there are two genders, and *cable* 'cable' is said to belong to a different gender from *table* 'table', simply because it controls different agreements, as in the two sentences *le cable est long* 'the cable is long', and *la table est longue* 'the table is long'. Now in these two sentences both the first and the fourth words have controlled agreements, and it would be to mistake the true nature of the gender to say that *le* is the sign of the gender of *cable*, and *la* of the gender of *table*. This may be plainly seen from the fact that the agreements they control are not affected even when they are preceded by an invariable like *l'autre* as in, *l'autre cable est long* 'the other cable is long', and, *l'autre table est longue* 'the other table is long'. This means then that *cable* and *table* belong to different genders, but that there is no sign whatever of this within the words themselves. In Latin, on the other hand, the sign of the gender very frequently is found within the word, as in, *mensa est longa* 'the table is long', where *mensa* is able to control the agreement *-a* in *longa* just because it has the gender sign *-a* itself.

The part played by gender in Bantu languages is thus seen to be somewhat similar to that in Latin[1] but quite different from that in French. The very fact that **-séle** cannot occur unless preceded by some element such as **-ci-** or **-mu-** proves that these elements are not agreements controlled by the gender, but the actual sign of the gender itself. For this reason they must be an integral part of the piece whose gender they indicate, so there cannot be a break after them.

There remains then the question of the first syllable of the segment. Are **i-** and **u-** distinct pieces or not? Unless they can be shown to have a recognizable grammatical function there can be no justification for treating them as pieces. It happens that this question can be satisfactorily answered by comparing the following sentence with (c): (e) **ciitúmba cíi-tálí** 'the big bag is a long one'. The difference between **í-cisélé** in (c) and **ciitúmba** in (e) can be shown to consist in the difference in the length of the vowel in the concordial element. What is significant for our present investigation is the fact that when the vowel is short, then the element **i-** cannot be omitted, but when the vowel is long, no such element ever occurs. This simply means that the initial syllable in (c) and (d) is merely a part of the concordial element, which is double in such cases, but single in (e).

What has been said about the independent concordial elements like **ici-** in **ícisélé** is equally applicable to the dependent elements, such as in (f) **cíi-séle í-ci-tálí** 'it is a long sandbank'. The concordial element **í-ci-** in **í-ci-tálí** is the sign of the gender of the segment just as the similar element in (c), and although this particular element is a controlled agreement, it can never be omitted, consequently it must be an integral part of the piece.

The only difference to be noted in considering stable nominal segments is that the concordial element is never double and usually contains a long vowel, as **cíi-séle** in (f) or **cíi-tálí** in (c). Since segments like these can control agreements (or have them controlled) in exactly the same way as the unstable ones, they must be treated as single pieces for the same reasons.

Our conclusions then with respect to nominal segments with one concordial element is that they are in fact single pieces and that no breaks occur within them. Here then is how the sentences we have been studying will be written: (c) **ícisélé cíitálí**, (d) **úmusélé úutálí**, (e) **ciitúmba cíitálí**.

(2) Segments with More than One Concordial Element

Two main types of these segments are found, and their grammatical function is distinct. They are: (i) Segments with two independent elements, (ii) Segments with one independent and one dependent element, or with two dependent elements. Since these two types are so distinct grammatically they have to be studied separately.

(i) *Two Independent Elements.* Here are two sentences for comparison: (a) **ícisíma cíitálí** 'the well is a deep (long) one', (b) **kú-cisíma kúutálí** 'to the well is a long way'. With respect to the grammatical relationship between the two main parts of the sentence, there is no essential difference between (a) and (b). The segment

---

[1] The important difference being that in Latin one and the same element serves both as the sign of gender and as the sign of case, as well as frequently indicating singular or plural. In Bantu, on the other hand, the concordial element serves only as a gender sign, as well as frequently indicating singular or plural. This difference is, however, not relevant to our argument.

kú-cisíma in (b) controls the agreement kúu- in kúutálí just as ícisíma in (a) controls the agreement cíi- in cíitálí. This can only mean that kú-cisíma belongs to a gender that controls the agreement kúu- in such sentences. But it has already been shown that if the gender sign can never be omitted it must be an integral part of the piece that belongs to the gender in question. There cannot therefore be a break after kú- in (b) which will have to be written, kúcisíma kúutálí.

The peculiarity of pieces like kúcisíma is their power of controlling two distinct agreements, or in other words the fact that they belong to two different genders at the same time. In the sentence (c) kúcisíma címbí kúutálí 'to the other well is a long way', kúcisíma controls the agreement cí- in címbí because it has the gender sign -ci-, and in addition it controls the agreement kúu- in kúutálí because it has the extra gender sign kú-.

The next question is one of grammatical identity, and it is raised by a sentence like this: (d) bá-lí-kú-cisíma 'they are over by the well'. We have to determine whether or not the segment kú-cisíma in (d) is the same thing as the piece kúcisíma in (b). The dictum that grammatical function is one of the most important criteria of identity has to be observed in this case. We have shown that kúcisíma in (b) is a distinct piece with the function of controlling two different agreements, so we have a clear test to apply to the segment in (d). Suppose then we compare the two following sentences: (e) bá-lí-kú-cisíma címbí ukúntu mú-léé-ya 'they are over by the other well to which you are going', (f) kú-lí-ícisíma címbí icíntu mú-lée-mó-ná 'there is another well which you will see'. For the moment the only thing that interests us in these sentences is the control of the agreements. It is clear that in (f) ícisíma, having one gender sign only, is controlling one kind of agreement only, viz. cí- in címbí and icí- in icíntu. In (e), on the other hand, kú-cisíma is controlling two distinct agreements, viz. cí- in címbí because it has the gender sign -ci-, and ukú- in ukúntu because it has the extra gender sign kú-. It should be noted that this well-defined grammatical function is in spite of the 'adverbial' duty of both kú-cisíma and ukúntu. Our conclusion then is that kú-cisíma in (e) has the same power of controlling two different agreements as kúcisíma in (c), consequently we have to treat the two as identical, which means writing kú- as an integral part of the piece in both cases, so (e) will be written bá-lí-kúcisíma.

There are also some other segments with a similar grammatical behaviour which nevertheless present an additional problem. Here is an example of one of them: (g) mú-li-ciitúmba címbí múúsumá 'in the other big bag is a good place'. The segment mú-li-ciitúmba is controlling two different agreements, cí- in címbí because it has the gender sign -cii-, and múú- in múúsumá because it has the extra gender sign mú-. Its grammatical behaviour is therefore identical with that of the first piece in, (h) múcibúmba címbí múúsumá 'along the other wall is a good place'. As there is no break in múcibúmba, there cannot be one in mú-li-ciitúmba, since we cannot separate a gender sign from the piece to which it belongs. We therefore must write (g) múliciitúmba címbí múúsumá. This then raises the question of the presence of -li- in this piece. As was noted in section (1), some nominals have a double concordial element, as íci- in ícibúmba, and others have a single element, as cii- in ciitúmba. Investigation shows that when an extra gender sign such as kú- or mú- is used, -li- is only present when the simple nominal cannot have a double gender sign; in other words -li- serves as a link between the two gender signs, except where the extra element takes the place of an initial syllable. Another example of the use of -li- in this way is seen in (k) **pálicímbí páásumá** 'on the other one (e.g. **icipúná** "stool") is a good place'. This therefore establishes that the syllable -li- in pieces of this kind has no grammatical significance, but its presence is determined by the nature of the main concordial element.

(ii) *One Dependent and One Independent Element or Two Dependent Elements.* Here is an example of a sentence containing a segment that has one dependent and one independent concordial element: (m) **icilímí-cí-á-muelé cíitálí** 'the blade of the knife is a long one'. It is clear that the nominal **icilímí** having the gender sign **ici-** is controlling the agreement **-cí-** in **-cí-á-muelé** as well as **cíi-** in **cíitálí**. This fact is clearly seen by comparing (m) with the following sentence which has different agreements: (n) **ifilímí-fí-á-mielé fíitálí** 'the blades of the knives are long ones'. The first problem then is to determine whether there are any breaks in the segment **-cí-á-muelé**. The element **-a-** is always preceded by a dependent concordial element which can neither be separated from it nor omitted. There can therefore be no break at the first of the junctions in this segment.

The junction following **-a-** requires more consideration. The first thing to note is that **-muelé** is similar to part of **úmuelé** . . . 'the knife . . .' or of **kúmuelé** . . . 'by means of the knife . . .'. More important, however, is the fact that the two parts of the segment cannot be displaced without a disturbance of the grammatical structure of the sentence. This is because a small segment like **-cia-** only occurs before a nominal or a part of a nominal, such as **-muelé** is of **úmuelé**; it is impossible to insert a piece like **naŋgu** 'maybe' at such a junction. The test of interpolation in other respects is, however, inconclusive, since a piece like **úmbí** 'another one' can apparently be inserted after **-cia-**, as in (p) **icilímí-cíá-úmbí-muelé cíitálí** 'the blade of the other knife is a long one'. It will be seen that nothing can be deduced from a comparison of (m) and (p), since if there is a break after **-cia-** then the insertion of **úmbí** is straightforward, and if there is not then **-cíáúmbí-** in (p) exactly corresponds to **-cíámuelé-**. There is, however, the question of grammatical agreement to be taken into account. The element **-cí-** in **-cíá-muelé-** is the gender sign of some nominal that is brought into agreement with **icilímí-**, by means of it. Such a piece cannot be less than **-cíámuelé**, since the gender sign is never outside the piece to which it belongs. If then there is no break in **-cíámuelé**, there is the question of the grammatical significance of **-a-**. The answer to this appears to be that it merely serves to link the extra dependent concordial element **-cí-** to the main independent concordial element **-mu-**, which explains why **-a-** never occurs without an immediately preceding dependent concordial element. The conclusion we reach therefore is that there is no break within **-cíámuelé**, which is a nominal segment with two genders, that indicated by the first concordial element being a controlled gender.

A further problem relates to the junction between **icilímí-** and **-cíámuelé**. We cannot apply the principle of isolation, even though there does exist the stable nominal **cíámuelé** 'it is that (e.g. **icilímí** "blade") of the knife'. The grammatical function of these two segments is so different that they could not possibly be the same thing. As in so many other cases, the test of interpolation yields inconclusive results. It is possible to insert a piece like **címbí** 'another one', as in (q) **icilímí-címbí-cíámuelé** cíitáli 'the other blade of the knife is a long one'. But whatever arguments may be applied for the presence or absence of a break before **-ciámuelé** in (*m*) are equally applicable to the corresponding junction in (*q*). A very significant feature is that no omission or interruption of **ícilímí-** is possible. If we attempt such a change in the sentence, we immediately get a different form in the segment we are studying, as in (*r*) **ícilímí, í-ciámuelé cíitáli** 'the blade, that of the knife is a long one', or (*s*) **í-ciámuelé ícilímí cíitáli** 'that of the knife, the blade, it is a long one'. It seems clear therefore that though in some sentences a break occurs after a segment like **ícilímí**, there is not one in (*m*). We are thus confronted with a new kind of piece, one which contains two quite different lexical parts, with concordial elements in each part as well. The important fact about pieces of this kind is that the first half is a distinct piece in other sentences. For this reason we are compelled to regard the junction between **ícilímí-** and **-ciámuelé** as something different from the internal junctions of either of the segments, even though it is not a break. It will be convenient to call this an 'open junction', and to indicate its occurrence by the use of a tilde. Wherever the two parts of a compound nominal display grammatical agreement, we shall term them 'temporary compounds'. As a result of these conclusions we shall write (*m*) as **ícilímí~ciámuelé cíitáli**, and (*q*) as **ícilímí címbí~ciámuelé cíitáli**.[1]

There are other less complex but grammatically comparable segments which behave identically and so must receive identical treatment. The two following sentences contain examples of such segments: **ícilímí~ciáúkó cíitáli** 'its (e.g. the knife's) blade is a long one'; **ícilímí~ciákúe cíitáli** 'his (e.g. the child's) is a long one'.

There are two things which result from the use of the tilde to separate the parts of a temporary compound. In the first place there may arise a chain of more than two parts, as, for example, in **cíilímí~ciámuelé~úámulúnsí** 'it is the blade of the hunter's knife'. It may be noted in passing that this does not happen in **cíilímí~ ciámuelé íciámulúnsí** 'it is the hunter's knife blade'. A further peculiar feature is the 'floating' tilde, as, for example, in **cíikopo~ naŋgu cíilolá~ciámúlímí** 'it is the tin or the mirror of the cultivator'. It is interesting to reflect that even in English

---

[1] The similar problem in languages where the grammatical behaviour is not the same as in Bemba will naturally have to be handled differently. It does seem, however, that this very unexpected result of the technique of sentence division, i.e. the existence of temporary compounds, is a characteristic of most if not all Bantu languages. In Swahili, for example, the shape of **vyawatoto** happens to be the same in these two sentences, **visu-vyawatoto ni-vikubwa** 'the children's knives are big ones', **vyawatoto ni-vikubwa** 'the children's (e.g. **visu** "knives") are big ones'. Nevertheless, the significant thing is that in the first sentence **visu-** can neither be interrupted nor separated from **-vyawatoto** without altering the structure of the sentence. However much we may desire to make a break before segments like **-vyawatoto** is seems impossible to discover any valid reason for doing so. It is interesting to find again and again in works on Bantu languages statements like: 'all genitives immediately follow the noun of the thing possessed'. If, however, these two 'words' are really a single piece, then such an observation is superfluous. It is highly likely that most Bantuists will feel unwilling to accept the fact that a 'noun' and a 'genitive' form a single 'word'. However, the whole point of the method used in this study is that we must accept whatever facts emerge from the investigation. This is surely the only valid method, and it is inconceivable that decisions on language problems should continue to be dictated by the instinctive likes and dislikes of the individual investigator.

examples of similar uses of hyphens occur, e.g. 'it is to the north-north-east of here'; 'it was a cart- or a dray-horse'. In each of these cases the omission of the first hyphen would produce a different sentence.

There is one other common type of nominal segment which contains two distinct concordial elements. Here is a sentence containing one of them: (*t*) **kú-lí-umúséké-na-amásaká-mó** 'there is a basket with kaffircorn in it'. The last element in this sentence is peculiar in two ways. It is one of a short series consisting of **-pó, -kó,** and **-mó**, which is clearly related to the extra independent gender signs **pá-, kú-,** and **mú-**, but it is difficult to observe the former kind entering into grammatical agreement with some other piece. Moreover, the elements **-pó, -kó,** and **-mó** are unusual in that the consonant alone serves as the concordial sign. With respect to the junction before the final element in (*t*) the most important fact is that nothing can be interpolated at this point. Thus if the piece **áyaiŋgí** 'much' agreeing with **-amásaká-** be added, it must be placed after **-mó**. It is possible to omit **-mó**, but then we find that the sentence is not the same, since the omission of the final element alters the power of the sentence to undergo rearrangement, e.g. **kú-lí-amásaká-na-umúséké** 'there is kaffircorn and a basket'. The indications therefore are that there is no break before **-mó** in (*t*), nevertheless the segment **-amásaká-mó** has several peculiar features. There are two concordial elements, **-ama-** and **-m-** with a lexical element **-saká-** between them; in addition the omission of **-mó**, while it alters the grammatical possibilities of the segment, nevertheless does not completely disrupt it. For this reason it is reasonable to regard the segment as a kind of compound piece, but as this is a new kind of junction we shall use a dot as, **-amásaká·mó**. Since there is no grammatical agreement between the two parts of the compound, we shall call this a 'semi-open' junction.

(iii) *Other Kinds of Segments with More than Two Concordial Elements.* One of the simplest of these segments is in fact a combination of the two main types already studied, as in **ifíúmbu-fíá-mú-mábálá fíísumá** 'the potatoes in the gardens are good ones'. By applying the arguments developed in the two previous sub-sections we obtain the following result: **ifíúmbu-fíámúmábálá fíísumá**.

A still more complex kind of segment occurs in this sentence: **pá-cíákúmúsébó páásumá** 'on that (e.g. **icísikí** "tree-stump") by the road is a good place'. Here the segment contains four distinct gender signs, **pa-, -ku-,** and **-mu-** which are independent, and **-ci-** which is dependent. Since, however, we cannot leave a gender sign unattached there cannot be any breaks in this long segment. We therefore have to write **pácíákúmúsébó páásumá**.

(3) *Segments limited by a Non-Concordial Element*

In addition to the nominal segments studied in the two preceding sections, others occur in which a non-concordial element occurs either at the beginning or at the end. It is simplest to consider these two different types separately.

(*a*) The segments with an initial element that does not operate within the concord system are of two main types, stable and unstable.

(i) Here is a sentence containing one common type of stable segment of this kind: (*a*) **cilíá-ní-ciitúmba** 'that one is a big bag'. As the segment **-ní-ciitúmba** can be isolated, and the two parts of the sentence can be transposed without changing the grammatical relationships, there must be a break before -ní-. When we study the stable segment ní-ciitúmba, we find that ní- can never be omitted or displaced. Moreover, the only kind of piece that can be interpolated at the junction is one which is grammatically comparable with -ciitúmba, as in (b) ní-címó ciitúmba 'it is one of the big bags'. Since then the same arguments are applicable to the junction between ní- and -címó in (b) as to that between ní- and -ciitúmbá in (a), the interpolation of címó gives no indication as to whether or not there is a break after ní-. It is when we consider the grammatical function of ní- that we discover that it cannot possibly be a distinct piece. Investigation shows that ní- only occurs in junction with a gender sign which cannot be dissyllabic, as cii- in ciitúmba or cí- in címó. Since therefore ní- is never found in junction with gender signs like the -ci- in ícibúmba, its occurrence is clearly determined by the nature of the concordial element. This means that we have to regard ní- as a morphological element which serves to strengthen certain types of concordial elements in stable nominals, since it is found that cíibúmba 'it is a wall', and ní-ciitúmba 'it is a big-bag' are grammatically comparable, and have in fact identical function.[1]

There are two other series of stable nominal segments which commence with a non-concordial element, but these differ from the ones with ní- in that the element occurs in junction with concordial elements of all kinds. Here are some examples with the element tee-: (c) téé-cibúmba 'it is not a wall', (d) téé-ciitúmba 'it is not a big bag'. From their grammatical behaviour it proves impossible to discover any reasons for making a break after these elements, since their grammatical potentialities are almost identical with those of ní-. The one point in which they differ only confirms the decision that such elements are equally an integral part of the whole segment. When they occur in junction with a concordial element which may be double in other sentences, as, for example, -ci- in (c) (cf. ícibúmba cíitálí 'the wall is a high one'), then the concordial element is always single. This means that we cannot regard tee- as an element 'placed before' a nominal, since it actually displaces the first part of the double concordial element, and so must be regarded as entering into the very structure of the nominal itself. For these reasons we have to write (c) téécibúmba, (d) tééciitúmba.

(ii) The principal types of unstable segments of this kind are illustrated in these two sentences: (c) cíipúná-ŋga-úlukású 'it is a stool like a hoe', (d) múucélé-na-ubúúŋgá 'it is salt with flour'. Considering the junction at the first hyphen in these sentences, we find that segments of quite different kinds may immediately precede -ŋga- and -na-, as in (e) cí-lí-ŋga-úlukású 'it is like a hoe', (f) cí-á-pú-tú-la-ŋga-úlukású 'it has cut like a hoe'. This kind of behaviour makes it almost certain that there must be a break at the junction in question. The other junction, at the second hyphen, presents a quite different problem. In the traditional treatment of the

---

[1] In some languages, like Swahili, where a similar element ni- occurs, this last argument is inapplicable since there is only one kind of concordial element. Nevertheless, what was said about the fact that ni- cannot be omitted or displaced, and about the kind of piece that can be interpolated at the junction is equally valid in such languages. There is therefore no justification for making a break in such Swahili sentences as nivisu 'they are knives' or nivikubwa 'they are big ones'. The usual argument from English, which equates ni- with the verb 'to be', entirely overlooks the fact that no interpolation may occur, cf. labda nivisu 'they are probably knives', where labda could not possibly come between ni- and -visu in the same way that 'probably' comes between 'are' and 'knives' in the English sentence.

question of word-fusion it has proved difficult for the conjunctivist to adduce adequate reasons for 'joining' **ŋga-** and **na-** to what follows. For our purpose, however, the important thing is that there are no reasons whatever for separating these elements and treating them as separate pieces. They only occur in junction with segments which are functionally nominals, and no interruption or disturbance of the arrangement is possible. In the case of **na-** there is the further fact that in some sentences a segment like **na-ubúúŋgá** can be replaced with another such as **na-bó**, the two being grammatically equivalent. Here is an example: (*g*) **bá-lí-na-ubúúŋgá** 'they have the flour', (*h*) **bá-lí na-bó** 'they have it (e.g. the flour)'. Now **-bó** does not occur as a distinct piece anywhere else in the language, and here nothing whatever can be interpolated at the junction, so we cannot make a break in **na-bó**. If then we write **nabó** in (*h*) we have to write **naubúúŋgá** in (*g*) since these two segments are grammatically comparable. Our conclusion then is that there is no break after **na-** or **ŋga-** but that both of these elements form an integral part of the nominal with which they occur. We therefore have to write (*c*) **ciipúná ŋgaúlukású,** (*d*) **múucélé naubúúŋgá.**

(*b*) Nominal segments frequently end with an element **-nsí**, as in (*j*) **ciipúná-nsí** 'which stool is it?' Although this element does not operate within the concord system of the language, there appears to be no reason for making a break before it. The two important facts are that **-nsí** cannot be displaced, and that if another piece is used in agreement with **ciipúná-** it is not interpolated at the junction. As it happens, there is a distinct piece **nsí** 'what?', so we might be tempted to identify this with the element we are discussing, and treat the segment of sentence (*j*) as a compound of the type discussed in 4(*b*) below. It is, however, interesting to note that a concordial element like **·pó** always precedes **-nsí**, as in (*k*) **kú-lí-ícipúná·pó-nsí** 'which stool is there on it?' Our conclusion therefore is that **-nsí** enters into the structure of the nominal to which it is attached, and so forms a kind of compound with it, but that this compound is not identical with those studied in 4(*b*). We shall therefore retain the hyphen, since if **-nsí** is omitted we still have a complete piece.

Another kind of non-concordial element occurs at the end of nominal segments, and raises a different kind of problem. Here is an example of such a segment: (*m*) **ciisóté-fié** 'it is merely a hat'. In passing it may be observed that this sentence is different from (*n*) **ciisote-fié** 'it is a worthless hat', this consisting of a compound segment of the type to be discussed in 4(*b*). The peculiarity of the segment **-fié** is that it occurs in junction with almost any kind of piece, so the test of interpolation is not easy to apply. Nevertheless, if the distinct piece **címó** is added to (*m*) it will not come before **-fié**, e.g. (*p*) **ciisóté-fié címó** 'it is one hat merely'; there is, however, a possibility of using **-fié** with **címó** in other circumstances, e.g. (*q*) **kú-lí-címó-fié** 'there is one only'. Most tests, except that of transposition, give completely inconclusive results, since **-fié** must always be at the end of the segment, e.g. (*r*) **mú-lí-icisóté·mó-fié** 'there is merely a hat in it'. This may, on the other hand, be simply a question of the order of the pieces. On the other hand, having adopted the principle that segments are only to be separated if adequate reasons for the presence of a break can be found, we have to treat the segment in (*m*) as a single piece. Since then **-fié** can be completely omitted without disrupting the sentence, this is probably another example of a semi-open junction which should be represented by a dot.

(4) *Double Segments*

In our investigations up to this point several kinds of compound pieces have been discovered, but there remain other types of compound segments to be studied.

(*a*) First of all we study those double segments in which there is concordial agreement between the two segments. One kind of such segment has already been shown to be a compound nominal in section 2 (ii). Here is a sentence containing another kind: (*a*) **cilíá-cipúná cíísumá** 'that stool (e.g. the one you know) is a good one'. The junction at the hyphen is characterized by the fact that no interpolation or interruption is possible there. A further significant point is that while **-cipúná** can be omitted, **ciliá-** cannot be, since **cipúná** cannot stand at the head of a sentence. It is illuminating to contrast sentence (*a*) with the following one: (*b*) **ciliá-ícipúná cíísumá** 'that stool there is a good one'. In (*b*) interruption or interpolation at the hyphen would be quite normal, and **ciliá-** can be omitted without any disruption of the sentence. Clearly then although in (*b*) **ciliá** and **ícipúná** are distinct pieces, in (*a*) **ciliá-cipúná** is a single piece. As both of the parts of this piece have a concordial element, it is similar to the temporary compounds already established, so we shall write (*a*) **ciliá~cipúná cíísumá**, but (*b*) **ciliá ícipúná cíísumá**.

There are other double segments which are similar in some ways, except that the independent concordial element is in the first part. Here is an example: (*c*) **ícipúná-citálí cí-lí-kúnó** 'the *long* stool is here'. What was said about the double segment in sentence (*a*) is equally true of this one, and in addition there is also the following sentence for contrast: (*d*) **ícipúná-ícitálí cí-lí-kúnó** 'the long stool is here'. In (*d*) interruption or interpolation is possible at the hyphen, or the segment **ícipúná-** can be omitted, but in (*c*) none of these things may happen. Since, however, the second part of **ícipúná-citálí** may be omitted without disturbing the relationships of the sentence, this is similar to the other temporary compounds, and consequently a tilde must be used.

(*b*) The other kind of double segment differs in that there is no agreement between the two parts, which are nevertheless grammatically somewhat similar. Here is an example of a sentence containing one such segment: (*e*) **icíbambé-ncénjési cí-lí-kulíá** 'the clever enemy is over there'. The segment **-ncénjési** is clearly related in some way to the distinct piece **íncénjési** 'clever person'. There is, however, one very important difference between the function of the segment and the piece, since **-ncénjési** has no power of controlling any agreements, whereas **íncénjési** can control the agreement **í-**, as in (*f*) **icíbambé, íncénjési í-lí-kulíá** 'as for the enemy, the clever fellow is over there'. In the case of the double segment in (*e*) there is the further point that no interpolation is possible at the junction without disturbing the whole structure of the sentence, e.g. (*g*) **icíbambé icó ícicénjési cí-lí-kulíá** 'that clever enemy is over there'. Our conclusion therefore is that the double segment in (*e*) is a single piece, but since it consists of two parts, of which the second can be omitted without disruption, it has to be treated as a compound. As, however, the second part plays no part in the grammatical relationships of the sentence, we shall use a hyphen, not a tilde.

In addition to those already studied there is a very large range of double nominal segments that are completely inseparable in that the second part cannot be omitted. Here is a simple illustration of one of them: (*h*) **insála-bubénsí í-lí-kulíá** 'the pipit is over there'. Although the two parts of this double segment are presumably related respectively to **insálá** 'hunger', and **úbubénsí** 'termites', yet it is in no way analysable into these two pieces. From all other points of view, however, such a double segment is grammatically comparable to the compounds just discussed. It is the concordial element of the first part alone that is the gender sign of the whole piece, and the second part always has a single initial element, even when the related nominal has a double gender sign.

Note on Compound Nominals

During the investigation of the nominal segments several kinds of compound piece have been discovered, but they are not all of identical structure. The one thing that the compounds have in common, with the exception of the lexical ones just described, is that if the second part is omitted there is still a complete piece left.

In the compounds that contain an open junction the second part is always some kind of nominal, and the two parts are in grammatical agreement. In the compounds where a semi-open junction occurs the second part is a 'fragment'. The remaining kinds of compounds, in which a simple hyphen is used, are distinguished by the fact that the second part, though some kind of nominal, cannot control any agreement.

2. *Verbal Segments*

Many sentences in the language contain verbal segments in addition to nominals, and some contain no nominals at all. In investigating such segments for the purpose of discovering the existence of any breaks we shall classify them according to the complexity of their construction. The simplest kind of verbal segment consists of a lexical core with a 'tense' sign and a concordial element, so these are taken first. Other segments containing additional elements are then studied afterwards.

(1) *Simple Verbal Segments*

In some verbal segments the tense sign includes a negative element, so it is convenient to consider them separately. First of all then we investigate simple segments in which there is no negative element.

(*a*) Here is a sentence containing a verbal segment: (*a*) **abáléŋgé-bá-ka-pí-tá** 'the hunters will pass'. Now the segment **bá-ka-pí-tá** is stable, and in addition a transposition of this segment and the nominal **abáléŋgé** in no way affects the grammatical construction. There is clearly therefore a break before **-ba-**. Now when we investigate other similar segments, we soon find that there is a series to which this one belongs, and in it are others, such as **bá-ka-só-sá** 'they will say', and **bá-ka-lá-bá** 'they will forget'. From these examples it is clear that the lexical part of such segments is a fragment. Moreover, there is another series containing **bá-ka-pí-té** 'they should pass', **bá-ka-só-sé** 'they should speak', and **bá-ka-lá-bé** 'they should forget'. A comparison of these two series shows plainly that the unit common to the first member is **-pít-** (not **-pí-tá**), and to the others **-sós-** and **-láb-** respectively. These invariable units we term 'radicals', and since invariability is a characteristic of the radical, we shall write **bá-ka-pít-á** and **bá-ka-pít-é** for the two segments we have noted with the radical **-pít-**. Returning then to the segment from sentence (*a*), we find that it has to be contrasted with others such as **bá-la-pít-á** 'they regularly pass'. It is therefore clear that the tense sign of the segment we are studying is **-ka- -a**, and that each of these parts has to be known before the tense sign can be identified. This means that the junctions on each side of the radical have to be treated in the same way. Moreover, it is found that the potentialities of these two junctions are similar, in that at neither point is it possible to make an interruption or to insert a distinct piece.[1] In addition it is impossible to omit either the tense sign or the radical without destroying the sentence. We are therefore precluded from making a break either before or after the radical.

When we come to study the concordial element, the position is equally clear. This element is one that cannot be omitted, and in addition it is clearly the gender sign of the verbal segment. The first part of the tense sign is characterized by the fact that it must always be preceded by a concordial element of some kind, and so the junction between them cannot be a break. From whatever angle we view the question, no reasons at all can be discovered for separating the concordial element from the rest of the segment, so we have to write **bákapítá**.[2]

(*b*) Verbal segments that contain a negative element are of two kinds, one containing **ta-** and the other containing **-sí-**. Here are examples of sentences containing them: (*b*) **abáléŋgé ta-ba-a-ka-pít-é** 'the hunters will not pass', (*c*) **ebáleŋge ba-si-a-ka-pít-é** 'they are the hunters who will not pass'. Now it can be shown that in each of these segments the tense sign is **-aka- -é**, but such a sign never occurs without one of negative elements. We are therefore obliged to regard **ta- -aka- -é** and **-si- -aka- -é** as negative tense signs, each consisting of three parts, and consequently to treat all the junctions involved as of similar importance. In the case of **ta-** there is the further peculiar fact that this is never used when the concordial element is **n-**, e.g. (*d*) **n-si-akapité** 'I shall not pass', which shows plainly that the negative element is an integral part of the verbal. A further feature of the behaviour of **ta-** which confirms that it is not followed by a break is that no interpolation or interruption is possible at this point. We therefore have to write the two segments as **tabaakapíté** and **basiakapíté** respectively.

(*c*) Segments containing **-li-** have to be considered since they are peculiar in

---

[1] It is instructive to contrast this typical Bantu behaviour with what happens in languages like English or French. In English the sign of the so-called 'future' tense is 'will' or 'shall' followed by a part of the verb without suffix. It is, however, possible to separate these two with a complete word, as in 'they will probably pass'. In French also there is a parallel in the 'indefinite past', where the sign of the tense with a verb like *passer* and a subject like *ils* is *sont* together with a part of the verb ending in *-és*, as in *ils sont passés* 'they have passed'. Nevertheless, the two parts are separable by a complete word, as in *ils sont évidemment passés* 'they have evidently passed'.

[2] Apart from some of the languages of the extreme north-western part of the Bantu area, where more research is necessary before the problem can be resolved, the same arguments are valid for all Bantu languages. For example, in a language like Lozi, where verbal segments are conventionally broken into many fragments, there are no reasons for making a break of any kind in the verbal, **batáfita** 'they will pass'.

various ways. Unlike other verbals these segments are not stable, and in addition they never have a tense sign that includes a final element. Here is one example of a sentence containing such a segment: (d) **abáléŋgé-bá-lí-kúnó** 'the hunters are here'. Now there is a break after **abáléŋgé-** since this segment can be omitted or transposed with the rest of the sentence. The element **bá-** in **bá-lí-** is the concordial element, and so cannot be followed by a break, but this leaves the question of the junction following **bálí-**. The first thing we discover is that **-kúnó** cannot be omitted, since a sentence cannot end with **bálí**. Nevertheless, although **-kúnó** cannot be omitted, it can be replaced by other segments that are not grammatically comparable, e.g. (e) **bálí-abálondó** 'they are fishermen these days', (f) **bálí-náámafúmó** 'they have spears'. Moreover, the distinct piece **báónsé**[1] can be inserted after **bálí-** in each case. We therefore conclude that there is a break at this point, and write **bálí kúnó**, &c.

A more difficult but rarer case occurs in the following sentence: (g) **bálí-balondó** 'they are fishermen for the moment'. Now unlike the similar sentence (e), no interpolation of any kind is possible at the hyphen in (g). If we attempt to interpolate **báónsé**, then we get, (h) **bálí báónsé abálondó**, i.e. exactly the same as if we inserted **báónsé** into (e). Now it is found that a segment like **-balondó** with the single concordial element usually forms the second part of a compound piece, so we are naturally tempted to regard it as such in this case. The difficulty is that the two parts in (g) are not grammatically comparable, since **bálí-** is a verbal segment and **-balondó** is a nominal segment. However, the test of interpolation appears conclusive, so we should probably use a tilde at the junction, since there is grammatical agreement between the two parts.

(2) *Complex Verbal Segments*

The different kinds of complex verbal segments will be classified for our present purpose according to the grammatical function of the additional elements or parts.

(a) *Segments with two or more unrelated concordial elements*. Very commonly a verbal segment is found to contain another concordial element in addition to the one immediately preceding the tense sign. Such elements may occur initially, medially, or finally, and each type presents different problems.

(i) Here is an example of a sentence containing a verbal segment which commences with an additional concordial element: (a) **icíntú-í-co-bákatúmá cíísumá** 'the thing they will send is a good one'. Since **icíntú-** may be completely omitted without altering the structure of the sentence, it must be followed by a break, so we shall study the segment **í-co-bákatúmá**. The first part **í-co-** has a similar shape, but different tone-pattern, to the distinct piece **icó** 'that one', which also contains the curious concordial element **-ic-**. The segment **í-co-** in (a) is in some respects similar in its behaviour to the double concordial elements, since the element **e-** can displace the first syllable, as in (b) **é-co-bákatúmá** 'that is the one they will send'. Our problem then is to determine whether or not we are dealing with a segment which is verbal in some respects, but which can also behave as a nominal in others. The question

[1] **báónsé** is pronounced *bóónsé*.

receives a definite answer when (*a*) is compared with this sentence: (*c*) **íco abáléŋgé bákatúmá ciísumá** 'that which the hunters will send is a good one'. This shows that the interpolation of a complete piece after **íco** is possible, and that in consequence there must be a break at that point. We shall consequently regard **íco** as a distant piece, and write (*a*) **icíntú íco bákatúmá ciísumá**.[1]

(ii) Verbal segments with an extra concordial element immediately preceding the radical are also very common, as in (*d*) **icípusí ciísumá, tuka-cí-túmá** 'the pumpkin is a good one, we will send it'. The very position of this element in the middle of a segment means that it is impossible to make a break on either side of it without going contrary to the decisions already reached. There is, however, an additional consideration which actually serves to confirm those decisions. The function of **-cí-** in this segment is different from that of the gender signs, since it serves to limit the power of the segment to govern[2] nominals. Any verbal segment with such an element can only govern a nominal which has one of the gender signs, **ici-**, **ci-**, or **cii-**. This means then that **-ci-** is one of the signs of the function of the segment,[3] so there is no justification for breaking it off, even if this were physically possible. Consequently we have to write **bákacítúmá**.

(iii) The extra concordial elements which occur finally in verbal segments are identical in shape with those found in a similar position in nominals. Here is an example of one of them: (*e*) **múlí ámainsí**[4] **múcisímá, bákatápá-mó** 'there is water in the well, they will draw from it'. Here the element **-mó** is agreeing with the nominal **múcisíma**, but its grammatical function is different from that of the gender signs in that it can be omitted or replaced by a distinct piece, as in (*f*) **bákatápá mulíá** 'they will draw from that place'. The duty of **-mó** is to act as a substitute for **múcisíma**, but it has to be distinguished from **umó** in the following sentence, although that also is a kind of substitute: (*g*) **bákatápá umó** 'they will draw from there'. The important difference is that whereas in (*g*) it is possible to insert the distinct piece **ámainsí** between the two pieces, no such insertion can be made

---

[1] In some Bantu languages there are verbal segments with an extra initial concordial element which cannot be separated. In this case there is evidently no break following the element. Here is an illustration from Yao in which the established breaks are shown: **cindandá cíbacítolélé balendó ciacíjipi** 'the bed the travellers have brought is a short one'. Here **cí-** in the second piece is agreeing with **cindandá**, while **-ba-** is the main concordial element of the verbal; nevertheless, no interpolation between them is possible, but **balendó** which is controlling the agreement **-ba-** has to follow the verbal.

[2] The expression 'govern' does not imply that there is necessarily any sign of the governance. It is an important characteristic of Bantu languages that while nominals control agreements in every piece they govern, verbals govern nominals without either piece displaying any sign of the relationship, other than their relative positions in the sentence.

[3] In those languages where no such internal element occurs the situation may be different. For example in Kongo there is the sentence **kinzu kiambote, tubaka kio** 'the pot is a good one, we will take it'. Among other things, the fact that the last two pieces are able to be transposed shows them to be distinct pieces. There is therefore a clear difference between the function of **kio** in Kongo and that of **-ci-** in Bemba, in spite of the fact that they have a similar duty. The difference in function may be expressed by saying that whereas the presence of **-ci-** in a verbal in Bemba limits the power of the verbal to govern nominals without exhausting it, whereas the **kio** in Kongo does not limit the governing power of the verbal, it merely exhausts it, as does 'it' in the English sentence.

[4] **ámainsí** is pronounced *ámeenſí*.

before -mó, instead we have (*h*) **bákatápá-mó ámainsí** 'they will draw water from it' as the only possible form. Clearly then there is no break before **-mó**, but since the element can be omitted, and the remaining piece is complete with its own radical and tense sign, it is preferable to use a separating dot, as in the case of nominals.

(*b*) *Segments limited by a non-concordial element.* There are some verbal segments with an initial or final element that may be regarded as additional, but which does not operate within the concord system of the language.

(i) The commonest element that occurs initially in verbal segments is **ŋga-** as in (*j*) **ŋga-bááfíká, tukabuela** 'if they arrive, we will return'. It is possible to insert a nominal after **ŋga-** without disrupting the sentence, as in (*k*) **ŋga abáléŋgé bááfíká, tukabuela** 'if the hunters arrive, we will return'. Now if the two pieces **bááfíká** and **abáléŋgé** were grammatically comparable nothing could be deduced from this interpolation. Since, however, the pieces in question are grammatically distinct, the existence of (*k*) shows that **ŋga** is a distinct piece.[1]

An interesting contrast is provided by another element which also occurs initially in certain verbal segments, as in (*m*) **ŋgá-abásumíná** 'they might possibly agree'. In this case, however, we find that nothing whatever can be inserted after **ŋgá-** without completely changing the sentence. We therefore write **ŋgáabásumíná**.

(ii) The non-concordial elements found at the end of verbal segments are similar to those already observed in nominals. First of all there is **-nsí**, as in (*n*) **bákásita-nsí** 'what will they buy?' If **-nsí** is omitted then the function of the verbal is different, since by itself it can govern any nominal, but with **-nsí** that power is exhausted. If a nominal is inserted at the hyphen the potentialities of the sentence are again different, as in (*p*) **bákásita úmucélé-nsí** 'what salt will they buy?' In (*p*) **-nsí** can be omitted without affecting the power of the verbal to govern nominals, which shows that it is not playing the same part as in (*n*). A fact which further confirms the absence of a break before **-nsí** in (*n*) is that if a nominal with an extra concordial element is used it must always follow, as in **bákásita-nsí kúmúsí** 'what will they buy at the village?' As in the case of nominals therefore it appears that **-nsí** enters into the structure of the verbal with which it occurs, but since it is apparently attached to a complete piece, it will be written with a hyphen.

The other non-concordial element that occurs at the end of verbals is **-fíé**, as in (*q*) **ásitílé-fíé icísóté** 'he has merely bought a hat'. Since the presence of **-fíé** in no way affects the power of the verbal to govern nominals, it is quite different from any other element we have observed in this position. Now from the following sentence it might appear that it is possible to transpose **-fíé** and **icísóté**: (*r*) **ásitílé icísóté-fíé** 'he has bought a hat only'. It will be recalled, however, that **·fíé** occurs as an integral part of a nominal, so that (*r*) probably does not contain a transposition after all, a fact which is demonstrated by the existence of (*s*) **ásitílé-fíé icísóté·fíé** 'he has *merely* bought a *hat*'. Whatever test we apply, no adequate reasons can be found making a break before **-fíé**, but since this element is a fragment, we shall use a dot to separate it, as in the case of nominals.

[1] In some languages the corresponding element cannot be separated from the verbal, since no interpolation is possible. In that case it has to be treated as an integral part of the piece, e.g. **bi-** in Luba, **bádímí biafíka·bó** 'if the cultivators arrive'.

(c) *Segments containing two radicals.* A not uncommon type of complex verbal segment is composed of two parts, each containing a radical, but the first only having a concordial element. They may be divided into two kinds, according as the radicals in the two parts are identical or different.

(i) Here is an example of a complex segment with two different radicals: (*t*) **bááyísa-tápá ámainsí** 'they have drawn water at last'. This sentence has to be contrasted with the following: (*u*) **bááyísa kúkutápá ámainsí** 'they have come to draw water'. The segment **bááyísa-** in (*t*) might appear to be the same thing as the distinct piece **bááyísa** in (*u*), but the former cannot enter into combination with an element like **·kó** 'at it', whereas the latter can. If we attempt to use **·kó** in (*t*) it has to be placed after **-tápá**. Moreover, nothing except the recognized internal element **-yá-** agreeing with **ámainsí** can be inserted at the hyphen in (*t*), in contradistinction to the fact that many kinds of piece can be interpolated after **bááyísa** in (*u*). It is therefore clear that there is no break at the hyphen, but since each of the two parts contains a radical, it is preferable to retain the hyphen.

(ii) Segments containing identical radicals are less common, and in some ways present more difficulties. Here is an example of one of them: (*v*) **bááliminé-liminé amábálá** 'they certainly cultivated the gardens', but this must be contrasted with (*w*) **báálimá-líímé amábálá** 'they cultivated the gardens in fits and starts'. Investigation shows that the verbal in each sentence has the same tense sign, and since part of this occurs at the end in each case the segments are evidently single pieces. One important difference between these two types of verbal is that whereas in (*w*) the tense sign is normal, in (*v*) the second part, **-íné** in this case, is repeated. The shape of the second part of the tense sign in (*w*) is identical with that in **cíalípésíímé** 'it shimmered', where the radical is **-pesim-**. This means that, as such a behaviour is only found in extended radicals, the verbal in (*w*) is behaving as though it has the radical **-limalim-**, which is apparently the radical **-lim-** occurring twice with the anaptyctic vowel **-a-** between. The two-radical verbals like that in (*v*) are different in other respects too, since the part following the hyphen can be omitted without destroying the verbal. The same fact may be differently expressed by saying that it is always possible to replace a verbal like **bááliminé-liminé** by another like **bááliminé**; in the case of verbals like **báálimá-líímé**, on the other hand, such a replacement is frequently impossible. For example, **báápeká-pééké** 'they were restless' cannot be replaced by **báápekélé** since no such piece exists. We are therefore forced to the conclusion that **bááliminé-liminé** is related to **bááliminé**, whereas **báálimá-líímé** is not, but is a simple verbal. We shall therefore retain the hyphen in **bááliminé-liminé**, but not in **báálimálíímé**.

One curious feature arises from the fact that the anaptyctic vowel **-a-** in the radical **-limalim-** happens to be identical in shape with the second part of some tense signs. In some cases therefore the shape of the two different kinds of verbal may be identical, as in (*x*) **náabálimá-limá** 'they have certainly cultivated', and (*y*) **náabálimálimá** 'they have cultivated in fits and starts'. That these two verbals are in fact distinct is confirmed by the difference in the tones, the one in (*x*) being clearly related to the simple **náabálimá** 'they have cultivated'. In other tenses there is not even a tonal difference, nevertheless the hyphen will have to be retained in the one case, since the two pieces belong to quite different series.

III

The Phonetic Behaviour of the Pieces

In the second part of this study two main types of distinct piece have been established: the simple piece and the compound piece. In addition it has been shown that there are several kinds of compound piece, distinguished by the nature of their components. This means that we must now observe the difference, if any, in the behaviour of the various pieces. We shall also have to note whether there is any difference in the things that happen at the various types of junction.

It may perhaps be useful to refer again to what was said at the outset of this paper about the significance of phonetic features. Even if no differences in phonetic behaviour were found to occur, the pieces have already been established by the technique developed in the second part. The observations in this third part then are merely a confirmation of the results already achieved. Nevertheless, it sometimes happens, as in the case of the occurrence of certain tone-patterns, that phonetic behaviour provides a useful practical criterion, since it is correlated with established types of pieces.

There are four important features that we shall deal with separately: (1) vowel length, (2) consecutive high-tones, (3) indeterminate tones, (4) tone-patterns.

1. *Vowel Length*

Two distinguishable lengths of vowel occur in pronunciation, a shorter and a longer. It is found that the longer is never heard at the end of distinct pieces in normal speech, but may occur in almost any other position. Such longer vowels may be due to an essential difference of quantity or to the junction of two vowels belonging to different elements. Here are some examples of cases where there are vowels in junction: **úmuelé** 'knife', pronounced *úmweelé*; **fíapélá** 'they are used up', pr. *fyáápélá*. If, however, the second of the two vowels is at the end of a piece, then the rule stated above operates, as in **káápótúé** 'they are coins', pr. *káápótwé*; **áámpumia** 'he has spoken sarcastically to me', pr. *áámpumya*.

It is significant that the non-concordial element **tee-** which occurs initially in stable nominals has one of the longer vowels, e.g. **teémutúé** 'it is not a head', pr. *teémutwé*, thus showing that **tee-** does not behave as it would if it were a distinct piece. Nominals like **ífiamúlímí** 'those of the cultivator', pr. *ifyaamúlímí*, also display a phonetic behaviour that confirms our decision that there is no break after **ífia-**.

Junctions in compound nominals, other than the semi-open, behave in this respect like breaks, in that no longer vowel length is heard at the end of the first part of the compound, e.g. **imbósia-misééba** 'last heavy rain of season', pr. *imbóʃamisééba*. Where there is a semi-open junction, the preceding vowel may be long, just as before an internal one, e.g. **múúsíá·fíé** 'he is only a slave', pr. *múúʃááfyè*; **naumú-tófúé·kó** 'with lead on it', pr. *noomútófwééko̊*. It is instructive to compare the former of these examples with **múúsia-fíé** 'he is a worthless slave', pr. *múúʃafyé*, where **-fíé** is a nominal, and so is in open junction with the first part of the compound.

There is a striking difference in the pronunciation of the two kinds of verbals containing similar radicals. The following two examples should be compared: **alápeniapenia abántú** 'he certainly treats people as though they were mad', pr. *alápenyapenya*; **alápeniapenia ámainsó** 'he rolls his eyes about', pr. *alápenyaapenya*. Here again the open junction behaves like a break in respect to the behaviour of the length of the vowel immediately preceding it. Semi-open junctions behave like internal ones, just as in the case of nominals, e.g. **tukamufúmíá·mó** 'we will make him go out of it', pr. *tukamufúmyáámò*; **tuátúúsia·fié** 'we have merely rested', pr. *twàatúúʃaafyé*.

2. *Consecutive High-Tones*

When two high-tones occur in successive syllables, their behaviour depends entirely on the nature of the junction between the syllables. If the syllables belong to elements which regularly occur in junction within a single piece, then both tones are spoken on the same level. Here is an example: **tukabámóná kulíá** 'we shall see them over there'. An element like **-ba-** always occurs in junction with the radical, so since in this particular case there is a high-tone on both **-ba-** and the radical, the two tones are on the same pitch. Similarly it is significant that in a sentence like **níkúmúmáná ulíá** 'it is the place by that river' the first three syllables are always spoken on the same pitch. This is what would naturally follow from the fact that there is no break in the piece **níkúmúmáná**. The only important case where there is a difference in the level of the tone of adjacent syllables which have high-tones within a piece occurs when the elements formed by the syllables in question are usually separated by an interval of tone. In the first three syllables of a nominal with a double concordial element there is usually a double interval, as in **ámakóófi** 'fists'. If, however, the concordial element happens to consist of one syllable only, as in **íkóófi** 'fist', then the two high-tones become adjacent, and the second is spoken at a lower level, i.e. *íkòòfi*.

At all breaks there is a different behaviour. The commonest thing is for the first of two high-tones to be spoken on a lower level, e.g. **icípusí ciísumá** 'the pumpkin is a good one'. Here the tone of **-sí** is normally distinctly lower than that of **cíí-**. In certain conditions the two tones are spoken at the same level, but not with the first higher than the second.

At the junctions we have indicated by the use of a hyphen there is a still different behaviour. The second of two high-tones may be heard at a lower level than the first, but not at a higher level. Here are several examples to illustrate the point. (*a*) **pumbúmáínso** 'kind of beetle', pr. *puumbúméènso*. (*b*) **múúpení~úámulúnsí** 'it is the hunter's knife'. In this second case the two high-tones at the junction are commonly spoken at the same level, but also with the second one lower than the first. This behaviour agrees with the unexpected conclusion reached in the second part of this study, that there is no break at this point. (*c*) **taakacíté-cíté filíá** 'he will certainly not do those things'. In this piece the tones of the second component **-cité** are on a distinctly lower level than those of **-cíté-** before the hyphen. It is significant that this is not so in **taakacítácíté filíá** 'he will not do things in fits and starts', where, as was shown in the second part of this paper, there is no open junction. (*d*) **tukatúmákó kafúla** 'we will send the smith there', pr. *tukatúmákòkafúla*.

3. Indeterminate Tones

Certain types of element are found to have indeterminate tones, which means that they have no assignable tone of their own, but occur with one tone or another according to the tone of some other syllable within the piece. For example, in verbals with a radical like -bilil- the tone of -li- depends on that of the following syllable, with which it is always identical, as in **tukamubilila ínsalú** 'we will sew the cloth for him', and in **náatúmubilílá ínsalú** 'we have sewn the cloth for him'. This type of relationship between adjacent tones is confined to syllables within the same piece, as in **umúlondó** 'fisherman' and **úmuléndo** 'traveller', where the tones of **umu-** depend on that of the next syllable. It is therefore significant that the tone of **-fia-** in the following nominals is equally indeterminate: **ífiamúlondó** 'the fisherman's (things)', **ífíámuléndo** 'the traveller's (things)'. This behaviour agrees with the conclusion that there is not a break after **ifia-**.

In nominals which commence with **tee-** or **e-**, the first tone is also indeterminate, as in **teemúlondó** 'it is not a fisherman', **téémuléndo** 'it is not a traveller'. This tonal behaviour would not occur unless **tee-** were as integral a part of the piece as is the **u-** of the simple nominals.

4. Tone-Patterns

There are certain other facts about the tonal behaviour of the syllables within the pieces that are interesting for our present purpose. The most important of these is that certain nominals are found to occur with one of two different tone-patterns according to well-defined rules. Thus a nominal like **icisote** 'hat', for example, when a distinct piece has the same tone-pattern as in this sentence, **icísóté ciísumá** 'the hat is a good one'. When, however, it occurs as the first component of a compound nominal of any kind, there is a high-tone on the second syllable only, as in **icísote-cisumá cílí kulíá** 'the *good* hat is over there'. We shall therefore expect to find that this same pattern occurs in the so-called genitive relationships, and this is indeed the case, as in **icísote-cíámulúnsí ciísumá** 'the hunter's hat is a good one'. It is interesting to observe that compounds with **-nsí** also use this pattern, as in **icísote-nsí cílí kulíá** 'which hat is there?' Compounds in which a semi-open junction occurs on the other hand never use the second tone-pattern, as in **naicísóté·pó** 'with a hat on it', **icísóté·fíé** 'merely a hat'.[1] This is therefore the second time we have found semi-open and open junctions correlated with a different kind of phonetic behaviour. But it is interesting to note that whereas a semi-open junction is preceded by a tone-pattern that is otherwise the characteristic of a break, with respect to the length of the preceding vowel it is like an internal junction. An open junction, on the other hand, is preceded by a special tone-pattern, but with respect to the length of the preceding vowel it is like a break.

There are two other tonal features that are worth noting, since they relate to the two initial non-concordial elements **ní-** and **na-**. Whenever a nominal like **kalimá** 'cultivator' occurs in a piece with **ní-** prefixed, the tone of **ka-** is high, as in **níkálimá** 'it is a cultivator'. This tonal behaviour in which a high-tone is duplicated is very

---

[1] This is to be contrasted with **icísote-fíé** 'a worthless hat', where **-fíé** is a nominal forming a straightforward compound piece with an open junction.

common in Bemba, but only occurs within the piece; so its occurrence here confirms the fact that **ní-** is an integral part of the piece in which it occurs.

The other point concerning the tonal behaviour of **na-** is more peculiar. If a nominal that has no articulated prefix has two identical tones, then the nature of these tones depends on the context in which the piece occurs. If it is following a verbal that ends in a high-tone, then both its tones are high, but when it follows a verbal that does not end with a high-tone, then neither of its tones is high. Here is an example with **tuute** 'cassava': (*a*) **kúlí túúté** 'there is some cassava', (*b*) **takúli tuute** 'there is no cassava'. Now if the corresponding nominal with the concordial element **baa-** is used, this syllable also has the same tone as the rest of the piece, e.g. (*c*) **kúlí báátúúté** 'there are different kinds of cassava', (*d*) **takúli baatuute** 'there are not different kinds of cassava'. It is therefore interesting to find that in a sentence where **na-** occurs attached to a piece like **tuute**, this element also behaves tonally in the same way as **baa-**, e.g. (*e*) **tulí natuute** 'we have some cassava', (*f*) **tualí nátúúté** 'we had some cassava'. This is not surprising in view of the fact that **na-** is as integral a part of **natuute** as is **baa-** of **baatuute**.

CONCLUSION

This study has of necessity had to be a mere outline, since it is clearly impossible to exhaust the investigation of sentence division within such a compass. Nevertheless, it may fairly be claimed that it has demonstrated the possibility of applying a scientific method to this particular linguistic problem. By arguing from the known facts about the structure and grammatical potentialities of the sentence, it has proved possible to infer the existence within it of distinct pieces separated by breaks. The establishment of compound pieces requiring the use of tildes, dots,[1] and hyphens may seem to be a complication, but we can only accept things as we find them. Moreover, it has been shown that each of the different kinds of junction in compound pieces is correlated with a distinct phonetic behaviour.

Some readers may have felt that the statement in the opening paragraph of this paper that the problem admits of one solution only was at least optimistic. It is to be hoped that the development of the method will have done something to dispel such feelings. The grammatical system of Bantu languages is unusually regular, with respect both to the structure of words and sentences and to the phonological laws, so it is natural that if rightly investigated the problem of 'word-division' should yield a rational solution. If this contribution to Bantu language studies stimulates others to adopt an objective attitude to the many problems that still remain, then it will at least have served one useful purpose.

[1] In an 'everyday' spelling it might easily prove to be desirable to reduce the number of these separating signs. This could be achieved by general use of the hyphen not only for both types of open junction, but also for the semi-open.

For Product Safety Concerns and Information please contact our EU
representative GPSR@taylorandfrancis.com
Taylor & Francis Verlag GmbH, Kaufingerstraße 24, 80331 München, Germany